Ernie Boffa

Photo by Richard Harrington

Canadian Bush Pilot

Ernie Boffa

FLORENCE WHYARD

ALASKA NORTHWEST PUBLISHING COMPANY
Anchorage, Alaska

Library of Congress cataloging in publication data:
Whyard, Florence
   Ernie Boffa, Canadian bush pilot.
   1. Boffa, Ernie, 1904-   . 2. Bush pilots — Canada —
Biography. I.Title.
TL540.B623W49   1984   629.13 '092 '4   [B]   84-6395
ISBN 0-88240-264-1

Designer: Jon.Hersh
Cover: Photograph by Richard Harrington
Photographs: All photographs are from the Boffa family collection
   unless otherwise noted.

Alaska Northwest Publishing Company
Box 4-EEE, Anchorage, Alaska 99509

Printed in U.S.A.

CONTENTS

FOREWORD

If you're interested in flying, this is a book you'll enjoy. When I began my flying career in Canada's Northwest Territories, Ernie Boffa was a Very Important Person; he was an aviation pioneer with a tremendous amount of northern flying experience, and we wartime pilots were greenhorns in the North.

I remember losing the oil in the engine on my Fox Moth late in the fall while on floats and Ernie flew my floats from the Bush into Yellowknife during the winter . . . tied to the side of his Norseman! For nothing, of course! Ernie always knew what he could and what he could not do with a Norseman.

There's no way to get dual in a Fox Moth, with just a single seat for the pilot, and during my first winter Ernie Boffa taught me a lot about bush flying. He told me how to land on skis on hard, drifted snow and where to find shelter for the aircraft from the rock-hard snowdrifts that prevailed in the North, plus many other important points about the country.

As well as being an excellent pilot, Ernie had great bush sense and a good mechanical understanding of aircraft. He understood the lay of the country in every direction from Yellowknife, where the watersheds existed and other topographical features, and he was able to use this knowledge and experience successfully before the country was mapped.

Ernie Boffa was truly a great bush pilot and a legend in his time.

Max Ward, President
Wardair International
Edmonton, Alberta, Canada

vii

Preface

How the Boffa book got written

Flo Whyard used to cover Ernie Boffa's flying exploits out of Yellowknife, in Canada's Northwest Territories, writing for the *Yellowknife News of The North,* for CBC news, for *Edmonton Journal, Time* and other news magazines. That was more than 30 years ago. Because she worked hard at checking details and established a reputation for accuracy ("and no B.S." as Ernie says), Boffa didn't mind telling her about search and rescue flights, and even took her along on the famous Santa flight to Coppermine in 1948.

He never sought personal publicity and shunned headlines and awards. For example, he has never wanted membership in the flying halls of fame. That's why Flo wanted to write a book about him someday, and made him promise that if he ever sat still long enough to get it written, she could do the job.

At the end of 1978, when her term in the Yukon legislature was up, Flo got in touch with the Boffas again, retired by then and living in Los Angeles, and arranged to start work early in 1979. She and her husband Jim drove down, booked into a hotel nearby, and spent most of each day for the next two weeks working through Ernie's photo albums and scrapbooks, and recording his reminiscences on tape. They made a lot of mistakes.

"I'd never do it that way again," says Flo. "I didn't know enough to lead E.J.B. through it all chronologically; I just let him wander along, reminded of a story each time he looked at a snapshot, afraid to stop him or change his direction for fear he'd dry up or get annoyed. That meant I came home and spent hundreds of hours playing those tapes and taking verbatim notes, then sorting the notes into some chronological order, then starting to write from them. Hard work."

As the drafts of the first three chapters were typed she sent them down to Ernie to check for accuracy, but he didn't like editing on his own; he preferred to sit and talk it over and had to be prodded into dictating his notes or corrections to Nettie, who would then mail them back to Flo. His tape recorder was handy, but he didn't like using it. It was slow work, typing and retyping, but Flo was able to present the Boffas with the first six chapters (third and FINAL draft) for their golden wedding anniversary in November 1980.

Then there was another long gap in production, another trip to Los Angeles to work with Ernie, home again to more work from tapes, more drafting, correcting and redrafting. In Whitehorse, it was a spare-time project, with other demands taking priority.

Finally, spurred on by desperation after being elected mayor of Whitehorse in December 1981, Flo shut the door, took the phone off the hook and wound it all up in a week of steady sorting of notes, typing and rewriting. That was it. Whether Ernie liked it or not, she was through; being mayor meant no time to write books.

There had been a lot of writing of captions, sorting of hundreds of photos, photocopying of letters, newspaper clippings, logbooks, articles from scrapbooks through the Boffa years, and, finally, a professional typing of the entire manuscript, ready for mailing to publishers in the summer of 1982. In September it went to Alaska Northwest Publishing Company in Edmonds, Washington, and in October was accepted for publication.

"It's tough working with someone like Ernie, especially if you happen to be friends," says Flo Whyard. "I wanted him to approve the material and be happy about the book, but he wanted to clean it all up nicely and improve the sometimes-colorful language he used! You have to walk a tight rope to keep the right balance, when he cuts out the praise he deserves and you put it back in again. But we're still friends — I hope!"

ACKNOWLEDGMENTS

The author wishes to acknowledge special interest and support for this project from Canadian Pacific Airlines who provided transportation from Whitehorse to Los Angeles for one taping session with their former senior arctic pilot, Ernie Boffa. In addition, they permitted access to their historic files and scrapbooks, and reprinted a number of photographs from their company negatives. Special thanks go to J.G. McKeachie, Director of Public Relations, CPAir, and staff in the photo section in Vancouver.

Welcome support was also received from Richard and Lyn Harrington of Toronto, who generously provided files of their earlier stories and photos of Ernie Boffa during his Yellowknife days.

Northern bush pilots are better at flying than talking, or writing letters, but some of them took time to remember stories about flying with Boffa. Special thanks go to former CPAir Captain T.A. Tweed, who came up to Whitehorse to add his personal contribution to the Boffa story: Johnny Dennison, Mike Zubco and Tommy Clark opened their memory banks as well.

Down in Los Angeles, Nettie Boffa kept the project moving gently along, acting as secretary and script girl, digging out documents, old photos and most of all, names, dates and places from her infallible memory. Son Joe and son-in-law Gordon Hornby did their share of checking typed drafts mailed from the Yukon. Putting up with it all, over the years, copying photos, digging through files and generally aiding and abetting was Jim Whyard, who also paid the bills.

Flo Whyard
Whitehorse, Yukon Territory
January 3, 1983

To Nettie Boffa, who was always there.

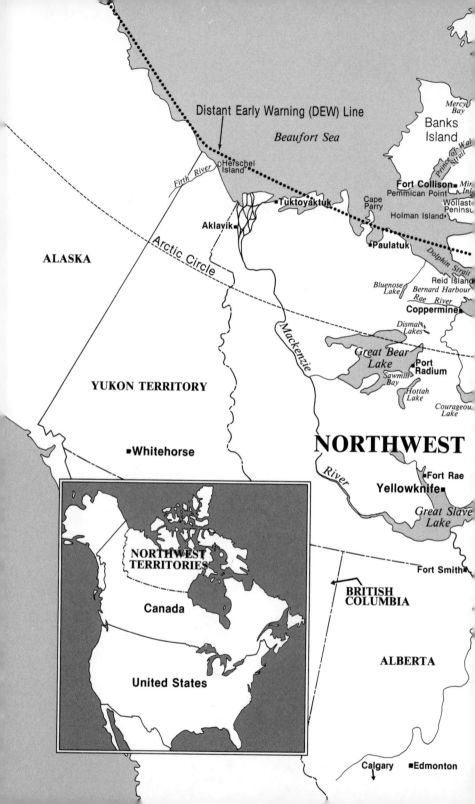

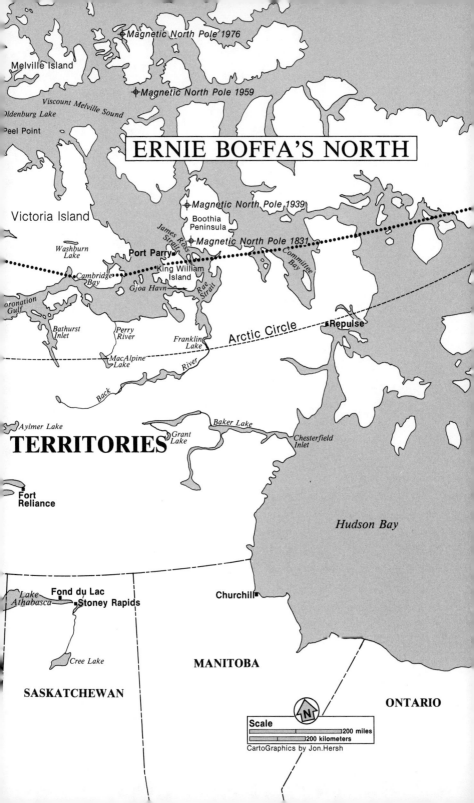

— 1 —
SANTA GOES NORTH

Ernie Boffa and I were flying north from Great Bear Lake and the dim December twilight was beginning to fade. It couldn't be much farther to Coppermine now. We had crossed the Arctic Circle some time ago, soon after taking off from Great Bear Lake, Ernie letting the Norseman drop ominously just to scare me, a sort of initiation on my first arctic flight in 1948.

But now he was serious, working the aircraft radio, calling the Coppermine Department of Transport radio crew, over and over again. No answer. He called again. Nothing but static came over the set. Trying to control my panic, I wondered what had gone wrong. Were we going to have a forced landing in this bleak white wilderness? I clung even tighter to the rope tied around the door handle of that Norseman. It was my job to hold the door shut and I needed no urging. It was -40° outside that door.

Finally, through the crackling on my headset, a voice was calling our plane, "CF-BHW," our Norseman's letters. It was the voice of one of the DOT boys at Coppermine!

"Where the hell have you guys been?" Ernie blasted them. "I've been calling for 15 minutes."

"Well, we're here now. So what do you want? Over."

"Tell me quick," said Capt. Ernie Boffa, senior arctic pilot for Canadian Pacific Airlines. "What were the names of Santa's reindeer? I can remember Prancer and Dancer and Donner and Blitzen, but what were the others?" There was a stunned silence and then a roar of laughter from that radio operator.

But Ernie Boffa really wanted to know. It bothered him not to have every little detail pinned down, neat and tidy. The reindeer names were important that day because we were bringing Santa Claus, with his sack of gifts, in that Norseman to delight the Eskimo children gathered at Coppermine for Christmas.

The story of how that trip came about is enough to make anyone believe in Santa Claus. It all began in December 1947 when the Daughters of the Midnight Sun, a social club formed by the first women living in the Old Town at Yellowknife, held a Christmas party. There were more than enough Christmas stockings for the few white children in the town and these, filled with candy and nuts and toys, and even a real, fresh orange, were turned over to the Roman Catholic priest in Yellowknife, the Reverend Father Gathy, to be given to the Indian children at their own Christmas party at the Dogrib Village nearby. Father Gathy invited his old friend Gerry Murphy to go along with him and be Santa.

Gerry Murphy was one of the best-liked pioneers in the Northwest Territories, a bachelor whose friends were many. He had a wonderful time playing Santa to those brown-eyed children, and

Gerry Murphy, sitting at right, loved playing Santa for Yellowknife youngsters, and hoped to do as much for Eskimo kids on the coast.

he decided there and then that the same thing should be done for the Eskimo kids at the coast. After all, Gerry argued, they should be Santa's very first customers, being neighbors, so to speak.

So for many months he worked on his plan to take Santa north on the next Christmas mail flight from Yellowknife to Coppermine. Canadian Pacific Airlines gave approval, and it was all shaping up nicely. Then, only a few short weeks before he was to make that special flight, Gerry Murphy died suddenly, having dinner with friends in the restaurant of the Ingraham Hotel where he lived.

Yellowknifers were in a state of shock when the news spread. Everyone knew this genial gentleman who had lived in the North and helped develop it for half of his 55 years. A veteran of World War I, then mining recorder at Fort Smith, Northwest Territories, he went off prospecting for himself and got into the mining business, and came to Yellowknife at the beginning of its gold rush boom. He stayed to watch it grow into a modern town 10 years later. Gerry had worked on the Canol Project (an oil pipe line from Norman Wells to Whitehorse, built during wartime construction of the Alaska Highway), helped establish a speedy route for war-time freight to Norman Wells, became first president of the Yellowknife Board of Trade and head of the local Canadian Legion. He had been working toward the construction of a community arena and had the satisfaction of seeing work start on that project shortly before he died.

Everyone agreed the Santa Claus flight should become a memorial to Gerry Murphy.

Down in Edmonton, Superintendent Wop May gave CPAir's word that the Santa flight was on. It would leave the second Saturday in December, with Capt. Ernie Boffa in charge. The Daughters of the Midnight Sun packed 50 very special Christmas stockings for the Eskimo children who would be gathered with their families at Coppermine for the holiday season. The Junior Red Cross kids in Yellowknife asked whether they might send fresh oranges to their friends farther north, and this special treat, carefully wrapped against freezing, was put in the toe of each stocking. Gifts for other residents of Coppermine were piling up with the Christmas mail from Outside.

The Christmas mail run was always the most eagerly anticipated flight of the year, as far as Coppermine people were concerned, but to have Santa on board as well made it extra special. The monthly "sched flight" depended upon weather to get through at times, and Captain Boffa had made history that year. As the Coppermine correspondent of *News of the North* reported, "Congratulations are extended to the personnel of Canadian Pacific Airlines and to Captain Boffa in particular, in having made history. The mail plane delivered mail every month in 1948, a schedule that has been unheard of before. Well done, Ernie!"

Down on ice-covered Yellowknife Bay, crewman Glenn McKinnon was loading sacks of mail, sleeping bags, emergency gear, and all the flying equipment needed for the flight into the BHW, one of CPA's two Norsemen. Under the critical eye of Captain Boffa the precious Christmas cargo of fresh fruit, green groceries, toys, candy, fresh eggs and meat was safely stowed away. Somewhere among all the parcels was a special package containing a complete Santa Claus outfit, borrowed from Hudson's Bay manager Sandy Scott. That just left room for Boffa, McKinnon, and me, a privileged passenger, signed on as temporary crew, to write the story. Our original Santa Claus, my husband Jim, was stuck out in the Bush on a survey job. Low temperatures and ice fog prevented his chartered plane from flying. He radioed into town from their camp, nobly telling us to go without him. And we did.

Full of good Scottish porridge and hot coffee served early that

3

morning in Nettie Boffa's kitchen (where I left our two-year-old daughter Mary Ellen in her tender care), I was bundled into long underwear, warm wool ski pants, sweaters and my white wolf parka. It was all I could do to climb the ladderlike steps up into the front seat of the Norseman next to Captain Boffa. There was no guesswork in his preflight cockpit ritual. We were heading into miles and miles of nothing but cold and snow and there would be no second chances. Even at the end of the 420 air miles to Coppermine, there would be no hangar, no ground crew, no facilities for aircraft.

It was bitterly cold that December morning. The temperature was slightly lower than we recognized officially for flying purposes, mindful of DOT regulations. Ernie had made two more last-minute trips to the Hudson's Bay store, and others around the rocky point overlooking Yellowknife Bay, where original settlers had built the first shacks, shopping for items requested by northerners on his previous run. One special request from the cook at Contact Lake camp, our first stop, had been for bottle caps. He must be making a brew, Ernie guessed with a grin, and would really need those bottle caps by now.

When we landed at the International Uranium camp to drop off mail and freight, however, he found he needn't have gone to all that trouble. The brew had been so successful that the cook had been in the sack for several days and was oblivious to our coming. Other members of the crew were doing the cooking. Nothing would have it but we must come up to the cookhouse for coffee and a bite of lunch before heading on.

We were served roast pork, nice and greasy sort of lukewarm. It didn't bother Ernie nor Glenn McKinnon, and I certainly couldn't let on that it bothered me. I hadn't dared tell anyone I was pregnant because Ernie would never have taken me on that trip, so I gulped and swallowed bravely.

At Contact Lake Ernie found his substitute Santa. He was Frank Legere from Montreal, known to one and all as Jo-Jo, and a wonderful Santa he made with his hearty voice and "Ho! Ho! Ho!" Only one little problem — he wore a thick black beard of his own, which gave us a small credibility problem later. In addition to Jo-Jo, at Contact Lake we loaded clumps of small evergreen trees, cut by the boys there earlier, thawed and tied together for Ernie to take to Coppermine. I wondered aloud whether it was emergency firewood, but Ernie laughed and explained it was a supply of Christmas trees for families at the coast, far beyond the treeline in Canada's North.

Second stop was at Port Radium to off-load more mail and

4

parcels for the people at the Eldorado uranium mine on Great Bear Lake. Then we were really on our way, with Jo-Jo and Glenn squashed into the back of the plane among trees and parcels and mailbags, prepping for Santa's role. That's what prompted Ernie's radio call; we were drilling Jo-Jo on *The Night Before Christmas* in case any of the children at Coppermine quizzed him. The radio operator told us everyone knew Santa was coming with us, and all the people had been working together to build a specially big snow house for the Santa Claus party. The excitement was mounting, on board the plane as well as in that arctic community that afternoon!

It was wintry dusk on one of the shortest days of the year when we circled the settlement, which I would never have spotted in that vast spread of white-on-white. But Ernie's trained eyes leaped like magnets to tiny dark dots which soon grew into half a dozen small buildings along the edge of frozen Coronation Gulf. I could just make out the white frame buildings: two missions, the Bay post, the Royal Canadian Mounted Police detachment, and DOT, as we made one quick pass over their roofs. Then, as we turned, I gasped at the fairy-tale scene below. A runway had been marked out on the rough ice by pink flares, and there were tiny figures jumping up and down, waving, in front of a huge white igloo, surrounded by more flares, some of them stuck on top of the snow roof, like a beautiful white birthday cake.

Still marveling at the sight, and craning for another glimpse through the frosted window of the plane, I discovered we were

Santa's first visit to Copperminers rated something special, so they built a giant snow house for the Santa Claus party. (Dick Connick)

5

down, bumping along the ice. Furry figures came running to grab the wingtips as Ernie gunned the Norseman for a parking turn. A final roar of the engine, then the ticking of the propeller, then silence. And outside the plane, shouts of welcome in English and Eskimo.

One of the RCMP boys rushed up before the crowd got too close and whisked our Santa-to-be away out of sight, with his costume and bag of goodies. Then we threw out the mailbags and hurried up to the transport building with perishables and parcels. It was bitterly cold; -30° with a stiff wind blowing off the arctic ice, and in the few minutes it took to run up to the post office I had frozen the tip of my nose. I didn't know it, but the RCMP constable beside me noticed and scooped up a handful of snow to rub on my face without any preliminaries.

But the Coppermine Eskimo families, warm in their wolverine and wolf-trimmed parkas and mukluks, waited patiently down on the ice beside the igloos they had built, happily excited about the whole affair. Up at the detachment, they were having a little trouble in the beard department, trying to stretch the white fur over the authentic black, curly one. But soon there was a dash down to the snow house by the jolly, red-garbed giant, who was followed by a laughing throng of happy people watching this fat man trying to scrape through the igloo entrance on his tummy, hauling a bulging bag of gifts.

Then we were all inside together, and there was complete bedlam. The air was soon blue with smoke from cigarettes and the gas lamp, and filled with human smells and that special odor of caribou hide

"Santa Legere," the tiny evergreens, and the gift-filled stockings all made Christmas magic for Coppermine Eskimo kids. (Dick Connick)

6

worn next to sweating bodies. The glare of the gas lamp set on an empty oil drum filled the igloo with brilliant light, but no brighter than the eyes of the children crowded around Santa. Their faces shone as much with pleasure as with sweat or seal oil, and there was constant squirming to get a better look at this mysterious Santa in his red suit and fur-trimmed cap, a Santa they had never seen before.

Little ones were picked up and held high by their parents. Out of their mothers' furry parkas popped infant heads with big brown eyes staring. Soon there were outstretched hands as Santa Legere opened his pack and handed out a Christmas stocking to each child. There were enough extras for those who couldn't come to the party and for other families expected in the settlement for the holiday. Mingled with the shouts of "Koyana! Koyana!" (Thank you! Thank you!) were shrieks of laughter from some of the men who had discovered the black beard underneath the white one.

Then it was over as quickly as it had started. Santa waved good-by, added a few more jolly Ho! Ho! Ho!s for good measure, made his awkward exit on hands and knees through the igloo passage and disappeared into the now dark arctic evening — strangely enough, in the direction of the RCMP detachment. Chattering and comparing gifts, the families drifted off to their own caribou-covered snow houses. Santa had delivered the goods.

The dozen or so white folk congregated at the post office to receive their precious Christmas mail. Here we divided the fresh produce I had brought along, feeling like Santa again. Invited to stay at the Anglican mission where we knew the Websters, we were sitting down to dinner there not much later. Three guesses. It was roast pork! Harold Webster's wife, Edie, had insisted on cooking the fresh meat we brought them, a real treat after months of frozen fish, caribou and the occasional canned ham. Once again, I could not explain why I wasn't very hungry.

Their daughter Marguerite, 10, was one of four white children that Christmas in Coppermine. Mary and Leo Manning at the Hudson's Bay post had two little girls, Maureen and Rosemary; at the Department of Transport station, Johnny and Dorothy Jackson had little three-year-old Patty. They had all enjoyed their first Santa Claus party.

Other white residents at Coppermine that Christmas included Walt Taylor at DOT; RCMP constables Martin Donnan and Dick Connick; Rev. Father Lapointe, the Oblate priest; Jack Scarlett of the Royal Canadian Corps of Signals; and nurse Dufresne and her husband at the federal Department of Health nursing station. That night they all gathered at the Mannings, ostensibly for a game

A windmill on the Arctic coast? It charges batteries that bring light to Coppermine's Anglican mission buildings. (Canon Harold Webster)

of bridge but really to hear all the news from Outside. We talked into the small hours, then crunched home to the Websters' over the wind-packed drifts of snow. My bed was my sleeping bag, stretched out on the battery box — the general size and shape of a coffin — a special Coppermine device. The batteries stored power generated by the big windmill outside the mission. Not a bad idea in a coastal community where the wind never seemed to stop blowing, apparently straight from the North Pole!

Early Sunday morning, brushing my teeth in the back kitchen, I was a sight of great interest to the first arrivals for services in the adjoining chapel. Eskimo families, once again complete with wriggling children, nursing babies and old grandparents, filled the small room to overflowing, lustily singing in their own dialect the hymns and traditional service of morning prayer. That evening in the same little chapel, the handful of white people followed the service for that Sunday in Advent, and Canon Webster led them in their favorite Christmas hymns in English as easily as he had joined in the Eskimo hymns.

Over at the RCMP detachment I watched, impressed, as Dick Connick prepared for a long patrol by dog team; in the police kitchen he processed 30 plates of frozen pork and beans, dozens of frozen doughnuts, bannock, frozen fish, hardtack and enough tea to wash it all down. At each stop along the way he could just grab an individual plate, thaw it out, and ring the dinner bell.

I enjoyed seeing the magnificent color slides taken on arctic patrols. Dick Connick became an expert on arctic survival, lecturing to Canadian Armed Forces and other groups.

The hospitality was warm but the wind was cold. Captain Boffa looked out the Websters' window and contentedly agreed there was far too strong a wind blowing that windmill even to consider taking off in BHW. That meant a Sunday evening gathered around the stove in the Anglican mission living rooms, swapping yarns . . . and learning fast. After the first embarrassing trip one grew accustomed to disturbing the conversational grouping to let down the ladder in the living room ceiling to climb up to the loft, and cat-walk along the center boards between stacks of provisions under the roof to the sanitary facility. Conversation carried on below until one returned, then the ladder was swung up again.

Coppermine Eskimos gather at the Signal Station for message time. The two whites are pilot Boffa and reporter Whyard. (Dick Connick)

On Monday we could delay no longer, wind or no wind. Captain Boffa had other scheds to fly with BHW. We had to say "Koyana, and good-by!"

The plane was lighter, heading south to drop Jo-Jo off at Contact Lake, and there was a sense of anticlimax. I knew somehow that I would never get back to Coppermine. Then, after we had droned for hours through the cold, gray day, Ernie reminded me that old friend Andy L'Heureux was the watchman for the winter at a mining camp at Hottah Lake just ahead. That brightened my day.

Andy was respected throughout the North by both native and white people. While trapping one winter near Dismal Lakes, he had come across some starving Eskimo families, and after giving them his own sparse supplies, had traveled at some risk to Coppermine to get help. As a result of this quiet heroism it was understood that

9

he had been granted a lifetime license to trap, just the same as a native of the Northwest Territories, and so far as we knew, no one else had ever received that special honor.

Boffa had stopped in on an earlier trip and lent Andy his .303 Savage to get a moose, and promised to come back before Christmas.

"Bet he's got a nice, fat moose by now," Boffa said as we headed for Hottah Lake. "Besides, we really should look in and make sure he's O.K. Old fella like that, all alone you know," and he grinned a wicked grin of anticipation. So the Norseman circled the cabin, from which a welcoming plume of smoke arose, and we landed on the snow-covered lake a few hundred yards away. By the time we had floundered through the deep snow to the path up to the cabin, Andy was out waving and hollering a welcome, a big smile greeting us.

"By golly, I figured you'd be along about now," he called to Ernie. "Sure good to see you. Come on in and have a bite. I got some real nice tender moose steaks thawed out, ready for the frying pan."

"No thanks, Andy," said that devil of a Boffa. "Can't stop today. Running short of time and got to get back to Yellowknife before dark. Just dropped in to see if you're O.K. and how the gun worked."

"Worked fine, Ernie. Got a real nice moose. Come on, it won't take but a minute. I been listening for you and everything is all hot and ready. Can't you stay just a little bit?"

"Well," drawled Boffa, letting himself be coaxed into doing exactly what he'd been planning since before leaving Coppermine. "Maybe just for a few minutes."

Then we were in that tiny, spotless room, and steaks were sizzling in melting canned butter, the coffee pot boiling over a roaring fire. We sat at a little shelf along the wall which served as a table, and northern chef and professional baker Andre L'Heureux dished up a gourmet's delight. The steaks, browned in golden butter, were so tender you cut them with the side of your fork. There was fresh homemade bread to soak up the juice, and hot black coffee. I had no problem being hungry at Hottah Lake!

Andy was ready to leave for Christmas at Fort Rae, on a trail he had traveled many times. He urged Ernie to take a nice moose roast or two home to Nettie, wished us all *"Joyeux Noel"* and waved us on our way. Ernie circled the cabin again after taking off and we could see Andy's tiny figure below, still happily waving. We never saw him again.

Andy L'Heureux reached Rae in time for Christmas, stayed a

The warmup is a preflight ritual in the arctic winter. Here, Boffa's plane is readied for the Yellowknife-Coppermine flight. (Jim Whyard)

couple of weeks visiting friends, then harnessed up his dogs and headed back to Hottah Lake camp. He never reached it. No one ever saw him again, nor did his dogs ever turn up. Ernie figured they went through the ice, crossing one of the streams.

But that December day in 1948, we waved cheerfully, our stomachs full of his good food, and his sincere welcome ringing in our ears. It was the same genuine warmth that had greeted us at Coppermine, and for the remaining moments of the flight, I indulged myself in memories of that exciting weekend, the happiness and Christmas joy which seemed so real among the people there. What a wonderful experience, to have flown with Boffa and BHW to Coppermine for Christmas . . .

Now we were on the last leg of the journey and BHW seemed to pick up speed, scenting home ground. We landed, unloaded the outbound mail and parcels, tied her down, drained the oil and headed for home in the pickup, moose roasts under Ernie's arm. Nettie met us at the door with her usual warm greeting, "Did you have a good trip? Will you stay and have supper?"

But I was anxious to collect small daughter Mary Ellen (who was most unwilling to leave!), get home, see my husband, tell him all about it, file the story to Edmonton and Toronto papers, tape it for CBC and tell the whole world about taking Santa to the kids at Coppermine.

Ernie grinned tolerantly at all this foolishness and settled down in his own comfortable chair, home for the evening with Nettie and the kids, the job done. There would be plenty more trips to Coppermine for him, and for BHW.

11

— 2 —
WHO IS THIS GUY?

S o, who is this Ernie Boffa?
It depends upon where you ask that question.
In Piotso, Italy, there are still relatives of his father and mother who remember little Ernie.

In Fort William, Ontario, he is still remembered as the builder and driver of the famous *Dreadnought,* the homemade racing car which cleaned up all the cash prizes on the circuit in the 1920s.

In Great Falls, Montana, he is part of the legend of pioneer aviation, not only licensed to fly there in 1927, but authorized to patch, repair and rebuild planes.

In Lethbridge, Alberta, he was one of the members of the barnstorming Flying Frolics in the hungry thirties.

In Prince Albert, Saskatchewan, during World War II, he patiently flew the trainer Moths, teaching hundreds of boys in air force blue how to get themselves safely up and down again, before they went overseas to save the world.

In Yellowknife, Northwest Territories, he was senior pilot for Canadian Pacific Air during the active postwar years of mining and exploration. He serviced the wartime source of uranium at Great Bear Lake's Eldorado Mine, and became famous for his uncanny ability to find his way in the uncharted Barren Lands.

In the Canadian Arctic, he was the man who selected and helped establish the first sites for the DEW (Distant Early Warning) line; flew the first x-ray team to Eskimo settlements; flew the VIPs from the Hudson's Bay on their aerial tours; sought out the historic sites of Sir John Franklin's expedition in the white wastes; brought out soapstone and polar bear skins to sell for the carvers and hunters.

He's the father and grandfather of Canadian and American pilots, the founder, with his wife Nettie, of a Boffa dynasty stretching west and north across Canada and from Alaska to California.

He's the man for whom they named a rum drink in the Mackenzie, and a lake in northern Saskatchewan, as well as one on Victoria Island's Wollaston Peninsula, and a street in Yellowknife, Northwest Territories.

Captain Ernie Boffa, who could "fix 'em and fly 'em," might land and wait out the weather, but he never aborted a flight.

He's a man with an aversion to uniforms, officialdom and any kind of humbug. He hates eating in restaurants and would rather bring everybody home to supper.

He's the original "Mr. Fix It," accustomed to earning his living through the years repairing bicycles, cars, and planes. Retired and living in Westwood, Los Angeles, he's still on call to "fix it, please" for family and friends for miles around.

Ernest Joseph Boffa, only son of Joseph and Catharine McCagno

14

Boffa, was born April 16, 1904, at Piotso, near Turin, in north-western Italy, in the foothills of the Alps. With his sisters he was brought to Canada in 1907 when his father headed west to seek his fortune in this exciting new land of opportunity. Egged on by a Calgary land speculator, Joseph moved ever farther north until he got as far as High River, working on farms but not owning them. Then it was back to Calgary, where he worked as a laborer and carpenter, building houses, two of which are still standing.

By 1914 unemployment and the depression forced his decision to return to Italy. Joseph Boffa was too proud to accept relief. He owned a bit of land in Italy and knew he could always make a living there somehow, though he would have preferred to stay in Canada. Taking Ernie and Carola with them, the Boffas left the two older girls, Nina and Mary, who had found husbands in Canada. They got back to Italy just as World War I started.

Joseph was a Canadian by now, and was determined to return to Canada. In 1915 he wangled space for his family on a ship which had brought horses to Italy for military use and was returning to the United States with a mixed cargo. There were two small guns mounted on deck for the dangerous voyage through the Mediterranean from Genoa to Naples, Palermo, Gibraltar, the Azores to coal up, and finally back to America. Young Ernie watched the crew engage in gun practice out in the Atlantic and wasn't terribly impressed by the merchant seamen. He acted as interpreter for some of the passengers during the trip.

This time the Boffas headed for Fort William, Ontario, at the head of the Great Lakes, where one of the sisters was established and there was work to be had. This was where Ernie Boffa grew up and made his first friends. He still has them.

Ernie had lost a year's schooling while away in Italy, and they put him back into grade seven at Fort William, despite his Italian studies. He quit school at the age of 14, the legal leaving age in Canada at that time, and got himself a full-time job in a bicycle shop, where he worked part time after school for some months.

"When I look back on it now, I can hardly believe it, knowing kids nowadays," Ernie says. "I worked all day and typed letters for the business at night. I ran the place when the owner was away and bossed the one other employee, a man 10 years older than me."

A few months later he was taken on as an apprentice in the machine shop of Canadian Car and Foundry, which was building 12 minesweepers for the French government, in 1918. There was a turnbasin upriver, Ernie remembers, and he also remembers that the last batch of minesweepers lost two of their number in a storm on Lake Superior.

Wooden ships, known as the Sault Series, were also built at the Fort William yards during the war and this gave Ernie a chance to work with shipbuilders from the Clyde shipyards in Scotland for three and a half years. He learned a lot and was close to completing his apprenticeship. At the end of the war he was working with an old Scot named Davie Kerr, who had his own little peculiarities in boat building. When Ernie wondered aloud about some of his sly tricks, old Davie would say, "Now lad, this'll no' be noticed when the boat's goin' full speed!"

They worked together on the two-hundred-foot *Kingsley* and built up a friendship of sorts. It was Davie who gave Ernie his first bottle of whiskey to take on a holiday outing with two of his friends, Red Coffey and Ernie ("Duke") Towell.

They camped out in an old, deserted lumber camp, and Ernie says, "We got drunk as hoot owls on that bottle of Five Star Scotch. There were lice in the cornflakes. You could hear them crawling around in the food box and we all got lousy. Hung out our sleeping bags and picked lice for three days, then went back to work. Some holiday!"

With the end of the war no more ships were needed overseas, and after the *Kingsley* was completed in 1919 the shop turned to building railway boxcars, then grain hoppers. The following year they were down to repairing boxcars. The plant closed in 1922.

Ernie had been going to night school, taking mechanical drawing, and at home he studied International Correspondence School courses in mechanical engineering. That went along fine until Ernie's missing mathematics was required. Dropping out of school hadn't helped. It got too tough, and he stopped struggling.

"I'm sorry now," Ernie says. "I could have been helped and I could have got through that course if I'd just asked someone for help, but I was too stubborn, and I didn't."

When Canadian Car closed they were down to three men in the machine shop: the manager, the master mechanic and Ernie Boffa. Working on their own, they acquired the rights to make York socket sets. Ernie made the dies, then the mechanic got the patent and went off to produce them at Lachine, Quebec, taking the dies with him. He asked Ernie to go along too, but young Boffa said, "No, thanks. I'm never going to punch a time clock or carry a lunch bucket again." And he never did.

Meanwhile, the owner of the bicycle shop where Ernie had started, Dolcetti, also owned and operated a garage in Fort William. He had the Hudson Essex and Reo automobile agencies, and was happy to give Ernie a job again, this time working on cars.

"Through that garage I entered a whole new world inhabited

by car-racing heroes," Ernie recalls. "Names like Frank Colosimo, Perry Davidson, Ken Campbell, Bert Bodani, who later became a member of the provincial legislature for Fort William. I was handy around the garage and they let me work on their racing cars. I remember the very first car I ever drove. It was a taxi, a J.I. Case, with an eagle standing on the globe on the radiator cap."

Young Boffa, left, with his 1914 Warren Detroit and crew, Stokes, Towell, and Coffey, were into auto racing in 1922.

A trip with Colosimo to Winnipeg, for the races at River Park, infected Boffa with the racing bug from which he never entirely recovered. With the garage supplying the parts, but working on his own time, young Boffa built the *Dreadnought,* which was to make him famous.

"It was a made-up car," Ernie explains. "I started with a Model-T frame, all underslung, very light. Then we put in a Dodge steering gear — it was stouter, you know — and an old Dodge 4 engine, with counterbalance crankshaft pressure, overhead 16 valve, Miller carburetor and magneto and what have you. Boy! Was that ever good! That thing was like a motorcycle. When you stepped on it, she'd snap your head back!

"Another guy, King, built a Liberty Ford, the type used at Indianapolis, and I drove it for him on the tracks at Superior, Winnipeg, and elsewhere. A World War I pilot, Slim Green, drove my *Dreadnought* and beat me once."

Ernie, the mechanic, remembers that the old Dodge had great big cylinders, four-and-a-half-inch bore, the whole head taken up by valves. They even cut into the diameter a little — each valve just cleared the cylinder. The Hudson Essex cars competed against Ernie's *Dreadnought,* driven by war heroes such as pilot Hector Dougall, one of the first bush pilots flying out of Winnipeg, who had started the first radio station at Fort William.

It was always a race against time, on or off the track.

Here's one of Ernie's hilarious tales. "Before I started racing myself, about 1923 at Capital Motors, we shipped up a car from Fort William to Winnipeg and worked on it. Frank Colosimo and I just had time to get to the track to get our guarantee to qualify for the race. He yelled at me to jump in and drive, so off we went.

"At the corner of Main Street, where you turn left to go to River Park, there was a traffic signal in the middle of the street, ringing

The Boffa-built **Dreadnought,** *with Dodge and other components on a Model T frame, made its place in auto-racing history.*

its bell, and I just made it around the signal, but skidded against the curb and bent an axle. Well, we just kept right on going, and pretty soon the police came after us. The motorcycle cop stopped us and was ready to take us to jail, right then and there. But we told him about the race, and talked him into leading the way for us — which he did, siren screaming, all the way to River Park.

"First thing we saw there was a four-cylinder Essex from Fort William, a guy we knew. We said, 'We need your axle!' He said, 'Take it!' And we pulled the cap off and got it changed just in time for Frank to get on the track and get our guarantee for the race.

Then the cop took us both to the police station. One of us had to get back to work, so we switched names — nobody knew the difference anyhow. One stayed and got fined; the other went home.''

Ernie had started out with Dolcetti, but after a year or two at his garage, he took off to visit his sister in Great Falls, and got a job with McKinney Motors, the Ford dealer there, for a few months. Then he came back to Fort William and this time went to work for Bodani, a former partner of Dolcetti's, at Fort William Motors. It was in that garage that young Boffa put together the *Dreadnought,* and it was logical that he should use a Dodge engine, because Bodani had the Dodge-Hupmobile agency. Here also he worked on Frank Colosimo's racing cars.

The *Dreadnought* stories could fill a scrapbook of their own. At the Lakehead it became part of racing history. Ernie Boffa got top billing as "King of the District Track Speedsters" in the local papers. One clipping from the summer of 1926, headed "Ernie Boffa Drives Fast Five Mile to Carry Away First Coin in Auto Meet," featured the following purple prose:

> *Ford Special and Red Devil give Dreadnought Great Chase in Closing Event. Local speed cars tore around the home saucer in clouds of dust to furnish a short but satisfying display of skillful driving in the holiday attraction at the Fair Grounds yesterday, in which the powerful Dreadnought, with Ernie Boffa at the wheel, shot home a winner.*
>
> *Close in its wake was the fast Ford Special with Frank Colosimo driving one of the best races since his Colosimo Special first went hay-wire, and the famous Red Devil was piloted by its fearless owner, Harry Davidson. For four laps in this dirt-flying and thrilling race, the Ford Special set the pace, finally to be sensationally overcome by the steadier Dreadnought with its nervy pilot . . . Boffa's time in the three-car wind-up over 5 miles was 6 minutes and 22 seconds, just 8 seconds outside the local course record. A crowd of about 1500 attended. The city sprinkling cart contributed fine work toward laying the dust. Not a few admissions were lost at the now-frequented free grandstand that the second river bridge affords.*

Freddie Edwards was the sports editor at the *Fort William Times-Journal* in those days and Ernie says he did a lot to build up interest — and admissions — at the races.

It wasn't all entirely disinterested enthusiasm either. Some of the sports writers were also the race promoters and it was of mutual benefit to promote attendance. Slim Green, a World War I pilot, who later became a well-known short-story writer, was at that time promoting the dirt track races, trying to accumulate enough cash to start an air service between Fort William and Duluth. Half the gate went to the promoters. The winning drivers got 50, 30, and 20 percent of the other half.

Ernie got fed up with all this by the spring of 1926, though he'd had some chances to go on the big-time dirt tracks.

"Red Coffey and I jumped on the train and left for Winnipeg with our tool boxes. We were broke. Rented a room from an old Irish landlady and celebrated my 22d birthday with two-for-a-quarter cigars. Happy birthday! We raced there on the first of July and beat the field with a Frontenac Ford conversion."

With that prize money they left Winnipeg to go booming through the west — Calgary, Edmonton — anywhere they could make a few bucks working on cars. Then, when it began to get cold, Ernie headed for Great Falls to visit his sister. He got room and board that winter for servicing his brother-in-law's fleet of trucks.

Then one day he saw a plane, flying out of the Vance Field at North Hill. That did it.

From then on life for Ernie Boffa meant flying.

— 3 —
UP HE GOES!

E arl Vance owned three planes and charged $20 per hour for
instruction. Ernie enrolled for a course of lessons, then got
a job at Pat's Body Works, which paid 75¢ per hour for
mechanics and $1 per hour for body work. With room and board
at his sister's home, Ernie put every cent he had into flying lessons.

He had eight different instructors, depending upon which pilot
for Western Air (later National Parks Airways) happened to be
around the airport when it was time for his lessons. Sometimes it
was even Earl Vance himself. Vance had been a World War I flying
instructor, and Ernie considered him a damn good pilot.

"Those were wonderful guys, those National Parks pilots," says
their 1927 pupil. "There was Nelson, Hollenbach, Stevenson,
Turner, Elsmore, Barnes, and of course Vance. Herb Holloway
of Vance Airways soloed me after 9 hours and 10 minutes'
instruction."

So it cost Ernie under $200 to reach his first solo flight — which
isn't a bad investment for a lifetime career.

After he soloed, every night after working in the garage at Great
Falls he'd go out to the Vance Field, just hang around and do any
little jobs that needed doing. He was a good mechanic so there was
always something he could turn his hand to. And he'd go along
with the pilots and the parachute jumpers whenever he could sneak
a ride.

"A farmer near Great Falls had a Waco, used it for barnstorming, and another guy was supposed to do a jump that night,
but I volunteered to do it for him. Let go over the lake and drifted
O.K., but landed very hard, and was bumped and bruised. Actually
I was happy to be alive. The next night when Vance saw me at the
field, he said, 'What's this about you doing a parachute jump? Do
you really want to fly that badly?' I told him I sure did, and Vance
said he'd give me $40 per month and 10 hours' flying time if I
wanted to work full time.

"I said, 'You got yourself a man.' And that's how I got started."

But Boffa was no flying genius, and admits having his first crack-
up, like nearly every flying student everywhere.

21

"Boy! I'm lucky I didn't get killed in that one. I was green, just like grass. I stalled. The engine kind of hesitated — didn't quit completely — that's what made me stall. I was doing a wingover. I didn't kick it fast enough and it stalled. I was heading for the ground and there was no control at all. Boy!

"But I knew right away what they'd kept telling me. *Push the stick ahead!* So I pushed the stick ahead and it took hold and I went over on my back, almost. Started to go that way, and I pulled her over, and smack! We hit the ground. Just got the nose up and she hit the ground. Banged the prop and undercarriage. It was the Waco OX5."

George Blend, left, and Boffa assess the damage to a wreckage near Great Falls, hoping they can restore and fly it.

Until he was licensed and could carry passengers, Ernie flew the airplanes from town to town with the barnstorming pilots, gassed them up, sold tickets to the crowds (if any) and counted the money each night back in a cheap hotel in the nearest town. They could carry three passengers at a time in the Stinson Detroiter that first year (1927), when they were barnstorming for eating money, and that meant $15 per trip. They had to cache 73 and 78 octane fuel all around the countryside for these ventures away from the home field.

In the winter of 1927-28, Ernie met an old Scandinavian carpenter who was building himself a replica of the *Spirit of St. Louis,* Charles Lindbergh's famous aircraft in which he had just made the first single-engine crossing of the Atlantic, alone. This old man had actually built the wings for Lindbergh's monoplane in San Diego, and from him Ernie proceeded to learn everything he could about wing work, rib spears, fabric, and aircraft dope. Boffa soaked up knowledge like a sponge and all of it was valuable to him in later years.

His first airplane, which he bought from Johnny Munssig in the spring of 1929 for $125, was a Waco 10 which had been piled up. Ernie worked on it in his spare time, at home and at the field, and by the spring of 1930 he had her flying and licensed.

Boffa's first plane, a Waco 10, he got as a wreck for $125 and put a year's spare-time work into the restoration.

During Ernie's time at Vance Field, Earl Vance went broke and took a job with National Parks Airways, flying from Great Falls to Salt Lake via Helena, Butte, Pocatello and Idaho Falls. They had the air mail contract and used a Fokker Super Universal for carrying passengers, and a Steerman for bad weather. It was all strictly visual contact flying in those days and there were no weather reports to help plan the flights. They had to fly through Wolf Creek Pass, a very high, narrow gap, between Great Falls and Salt Lake City. There was no room to turn around if you ran into trouble, so you really had to know in advance what the weather was like up there.

National Parks arranged to get their own weather report daily, from a man who lived in a cabin which looked across to that part of the pass. They would phone him, and if he could see the high part of the mountain only, they used the Fokker. If he could see only the low part, they used the Steerman. If he couldn't see either, they washed out the flight that day!

There was literally no mail at times. Nobody around Great Falls had caught on to the idea of sending letters by air. So Vance and the boys gave their new service a little nudge. Part of Ernie's job each day was to prepare five letters, address the five envelopes to one of the five stops en route, mark them AIR MAIL in large letters, then take them to the mail boxes around town and post them. That way they could be sure of a flight the next day! The odd air-mail letter would get lost in the regular, large blue official mailbags, so Vance and the crew sat down and stitched up some lighter, smaller bags to carry air mail only — probably, Ernie figures, the first such containers in the United States.

Great Falls had a smelter and power plant for ore shipped there from Butte for processing. The smelter had a brick smokestack 500 feet high, 50 feet across the top. The plume of smoke pouring out daily could be seen from Shelby, 75 miles away, but nobody was worried about pollution in those days. Ernie recalls that it made a great homing device because it was within a mile of Vance Field. It was also a great wind indicator and a very welcome sight at the end of a long flight. The prevailing wind was toward Havre, so it didn't bother the pilots using Vance Field. They were pretty relaxed about things anyway.

"Just to show you how relaxed everybody was," Ernie says, "I went to Havre to pick up a plane, a Commandair, for Louie Lee. So, of course, I wanted to test fly it first, because I'd never flown it before. I said to the guy who owned it he'd better come up with me because I figured it would be better to have him up front in case anything went wrong.

"So we went up and checked her out, and I brought her down again. Then I discovered there had been no control stick up front where he was! That guy just went up for the ride! I said, 'What the hell?' And he just said, 'I figured you'd be all right.' "

There was an Augusta, Montana, sheep rancher named Al Royston who had staked Vance when he started up his flying operation. Royston was flying a Stinson Junior, a four-place plane with a Wright J 62.25 with seven cylinders. Flying home to the ranch one day, he wiped out the undercarriage, so Ernie, McCartney and Felix, the roustabout grease monkey, were sent out to repair it. The plane's belly had been ripped open, so they tied in a plank, drilled holes in the plank, wired it to the fuselage, and flew her home from the ranch to the field. There was no such thing as a ferry inspection in those days — in fact, there were still unlicensed but legal pilots in some states.

Ernie went along with Royston once on a charter from Great Falls to Lethbridge in the Stinson. They wound up flat on their back at the airport in a bad wind, and broke the engine mounts. Ernie welded parts, v'ed the ends, put on hooks and turnbuckles, and they flew her home to Great Falls. Vance said it was "a good job," praise which Ernie still remembers.

Young pilots learned the hard way then, and they still do, Ernie says. Flying the Waco from Butte to Helena one day, the engine sprang a water leak. There was no place to land, so Ernie just kept going. About 10 or 15 miles from Helena Valley airport, the engine began to get hot. He was only a couple of thousand feet up when she started boiling — just about ready to seize up — then he went over the last hill and down into the airport.

"Boy! I was sweating blood that time," says Ernie.

But it wasn't all serious flying.

"There was this bootlegger named Chick Brown," Ernie grins, "who had a big plant at Sand Coulee, near Great Falls. He had bought an OX5 Eagle. He used to bring the booze in for all of us. We kept the OX5 at the field and I maintained it for him. One Sunday I was flying it with Chick and Frank Haddock, our parachute jumper, as passengers, when the first thing I knew, Haddock gets out on one wing and then stood right over and straddled the cockpit behind me! Then Chick Brown gets out on the other side! I'm hollering at these crazy nuts, yelling at them to get back in, but Chick didn't know it was really dangerous on that plane. Haddock knew better, and he finally got back in, so we stayed in the air. Clowns, those two!

"My brother-in-law, Mary's husband, operated a slaughterhouse at Great Falls, and Frank Haddock used to work there when he was broke, which was often. Chick would bring a gallon of moonshine along in his plane and parachute it down to Frank at the slaughterhouse. Chick was killed later, in a 225 Wright Whirlwind."

When things were quiet around Vance Field, Ernie was allowed to putter away at his own special projects. One day he was working on his Model-T Ford, hot and sweating, with the engine out. A tall man came around the corner and asked for Mr. Vance. Without bothering to look up Ernie said he was away and wouldn't be back for a couple of days.

"Oh," said the man, "I wanted to arrange to have him fly some of my guests out to the ranch." It was Gary Cooper. He often dropped in at the Great Falls field on his way to his Montana property and many Hollywood "greats" came for a visit during Ernie's time.

Glider flights were another attraction at Great Falls in those early days, and all the pilots took turns learning the hard way. They'd do anything new to get paying customers out to the field. One particular day it was Ernie's turn.

"It was kind of gusty, and we weren't too keen on flying this thing. Nobody had any training or instruction, you know, but we could all fly an airplane. So anyway, I said I'd do it. I got in and they gave me a short pull, a couple of guys on each side of this V with the long shock cord, pulling it like a slingshot. A couple of fellows are holding back on the glider . . . then they let her go. Up I went, not very high, just real nice . . . then on down again.

"So I said, 'Give me a good pull this time.' We were getting close to the edge of the hill and we had an upcurrent there. Of course we were looking for an upcurrent, but not quite so strong as it turned out to be! So when they gave me this great pull, I was really going up nicely, then WHAM! This gust hit me and the glider was just like a piece of paper. No control at all. So I kicked the rudder, came down, pulled her up, and sat down at an angle. And the wind's behind me, almost 180°. The wind is pushing up the tail of this glider. I've got this belt on, and I'm holding back with all my might, straining to keep this thing from going over and smashing to bits. The other guys are just running, you know, and it finally got away on me. I'll bet that rudder was a foot off the ground when they arrived and caught it! That was close enough, I'll tell you."

In the winter of 1929-30, Ernie was working at Great Falls when the United States Air Force put on a winter experiment to see how

In the winter of 1929-30 the U.S. Air Force had Curtiss Hawks on corrugated aluminum skis "scattered all across the state" of Montana.

26

The air force recruited everyone to help start the Hawks. Here the Great Falls steamer machine blows steam into a Hawk engine.

their Curtiss Hawk pursuit biplanes would function with their V12-cylinder, liquid-cooled engines. There were also several Ford Trimotors hauling the ground crew along on the exercises. What happened is now aviation history.

Here's Ernie's version. "They were all on metal skis, corrugated aluminum, and they scattered Curtiss Hawks all across the state, from Selfridge Field clear over to Great Falls. They started to stagger into Great Falls, which had two airports by then; Vance Field where I worked and then the town started one over on the other side, on the way to Helena. The air force boys were supposed to land at the town field, but one smart guy saw our beautiful brick hangar and our good facilities and our airplanes parked in line, so he decided to land at our place. We pulled him in and put him on wheels and tucked him away in the hangar.

"The others all ended up at the municipal field, ice dripping off their wings. The next day they recruited everybody to get these things started, including our crew from Vance Field, and the town steamer machine to blow steam down into the engines and get them warmed up. Of course we were used to winter flying, and we had fire pots. We collected all the pots we could scrounge. The planes at our field were always ready to go, started and warmed up by ten every morning.

"The others were frozen. They'd start this and they'd start that

27

and by the time all of them were ready to go it would be too late in the day to start out. So they'd drain everything down and over-night again. It was a nightmare, no fooling!

"I could have gone up in that little old Waco OX5, with a machine gun or a couple of little homemade bombs, and wiped out part of the U.S. Air Force!

"I remember the *Great Falls Tribune* had a picture of them in the paper, and the caption said, 'Waiting For the Chinook . . . With Apologies to Charlie Russell.' You remember that famous painting of the last of the cattle, all the others frozen, huddled together, waiting for a chinook? Well, that was pretty good. That's something the air force wouldn't particularly want anybody to remember, I guess."

By summer of 1928 Ernie had qualified as an air mechanic. By the fall of that year he had his private pilot's license. By the fall of 1929, after some more racing on the auto track at Fort William, he had earned his Limited Commercial License.

Then Ernie Boffa took his rebuilt Waco to Lethbridge, Alberta, got ready to write his Canadian Commerical Pilot tests, and passed them in August 1930.

— 4 —
THE HUNGRY THIRTIES

At Southern Alberta Airways, in Lethbridge, Boffa joined a group of Canadian pilots which included Charlie Elliott, George Ross, Louie Lee, Bob Kearn, and Charlie Tweed. By then his Waco 10 had been licensed to fly in Canada and Elliott flew it for him, as well as running a flying school in Medicine Hat. Ernie was busy patching up airplanes; the Gypsy Moth cracked up on July 1 that year, the same day the Curtiss Robin burned.

But Ernie wasn't too busy to spend some time with a pretty young girl named Nicholas McTaggart, who came from south of Lethbridge. "Nettie" was just 16 but already working away from home, and this bold young pilot was something new and exciting. She was a little bit older when they were married on November 25, 1930, and had perhaps some vague idea of what she was getting into, but she needed every bit of that youthful stamina and Scottish backbone to survive the next 50 years with Ernie Boffa. (They celebrated their golden wedding anniversary with family and friends at Edmonton in November 1980.)

Nettie didn't have a hope of turning him down anyway, because when she took him home to meet her family they all fell into the Boffa fan club. Nettie's brother, Andrew, followed Ernie into aviation years later, becoming chief maintenance supervisor for CPAir at Whitehorse.

Miss Katherine Stinson had been the first woman pilot to fly at Lethbridge, in 1918, but Mrs. Ernie Boffa became the first woman to learn to fly at Lethbridge, instructed by Charlie Tweed.

In those early days of the Canadian prairies, when there was little or no business for the airplanes, the boys would go looking for passengers. On Labor Day in 1930, even the holiday didn't attract the crowds to the Medicine Hat field for rides. Everybody was broke and business was rotten. That's when E.J.B. came up with this bright idea of having a wingwalker do more than his usual act; the stuntman would also perform on a trapeze down below the under-carriage. Ernie admits some of the inspiration came while the boys were sitting around the beer parlor. When nobody seemed too attracted by the idea he volunteered to do the stunt himself. To

29

advertise this great event, he recalls writing it on town sidewalks because they had no money for any other promotion.

Sobering up a little, Boffa realized he'd better get himself organized. He went over to the fire station where he knew a student pilot, Fergy Fraser, who was also a fireman (later a fire fighter with the RCAF), and borrowed his fireman's belt and hook. Then he went somewhere else and borrowed a lariat. His theory was that he would crawl down under the plane, hook the fireman's belt onto the loop of the rope, and then perform, supposedly hanging on by his teeth. Look, Ma, no hands!

A fair crowd gathered to watch this new trick. Up they went, with Louie Lee flying the plane, and Ernie doing his wingwalking. Then he climbed down the rope and went into his thrilling new routine. Everything worked just fine — until it was time to climb back up again. Then he found he couldn't make it.

The undercarriage was greasy, his hands greasy; no matter how hard he tried to pull himself up, he couldn't. He just got weaker the more he tried.

So he slid back down the rope, hooked onto the belt, and hung there while the plane flew around and around. Lee knew something was wrong, but not being able to see Ernie or communicate with him, Louie couldn't tell what had happened. Finally he decided to land and get it over with.

By now the crowd was getting its money's worth.

Ernie says he did a lot of fast thinking as they came in for that landing. He swung around to face the front as they got closer to the ground, then grabbed the rope as his running feet hit the ground — and was pulled along by the airplane, sliding on the grass. He admits he "bruised the knees a little bit." Those who were watching, transfixed, nearly had heart attacks, including Nettie. She still married him after that!

Postscript to that story: Years later, when Ernie was flying fish in northern Saskatchewan, he landed one day and walked into the camp cookhouse just as one of the men was telling how he had seen this incredible wingwalker and stuntman perform at Medicine Hat that Labor Day. He turned to the door, took one look and shouted, "And there he is, right now!"

When Ernie was flying out of Lethbridge, barnstorming with Roy Lumheim, who had been a friend of Nettie's before she met Boffa, they would head for Champion, Alberta, because there was a grain elevator man there who always bought a ride when the plane came around. That would give them enough money for some gas.

Then they would have to wait until the end of the working day for others to show up. Charlie Tweed's wife, Lillian, would make them some sandwiches to start out with, but by late afternoon they would be pretty hungry again. There'd usually be a few kids around, attracted when the plane landed in a nearby field, but they had no money to fly.

Ernie remembers: "Roy was good with kids. He'd talk to them and get them going, then he'd make them a deal. He'd say, 'You go home and get your mother to make us some sandwiches and we'll give you a ride in the airplane.' So the kid would run home and come back with something good for us to eat. Then when we got a paying passenger later, we'd throw the kid in too."

Many of the early pilots took turns at wingwalking and parachute jumping, so they had to know how to repack the chutes.

"We used cotton air chutes, called 'balloon' chutes, because they'd been used in observation balloons during World War I," Ernie remembers. "They were tied to the wing, packed in a bag, and had a sort of steering wheel with all the shroud lines tied to it. There were two snap hooks on it. You hooked onto your harness

Parachute jumping was one trick in the barnstormers' bag. Here they repack Lumheim's "balloon" chute with newspaper between the folds.

when you knelt out on the wing. You held on with one hand, hooked this on, and pulled the puckering string when the pilot shut off the engine. He would lift the tail — you didn't let go too soon. You'd sort of count — one-two-three — after he shut off, to slow down and get rid of the slipstream, you see. And then he'd lift the tail and you'd just let go and fall backward. It would pull the chute out of the bag. And when it opened, there'd be paper all over the

31

air. The balloon chute was easy to pack; you just put a sheet of newspaper between each fold.

"Then we had the backpack chutes we used for safety, Irwins. They were hard to repack, so we only used them for risky jobs like double jumps."

One particular jump Ernie and Roy never forgot.

"We were flying at Luceland, Saskatchewan, one day, and Roy Lumheim was doing the jumping. I noticed this first chute wasn't opening very fast that day. Maybe he was letting go too soon. But this particular day it had rained a bit, and everything was kind of moist. The chute was kind of damp; it felt, well, not really good and dry.

"And I said, 'Butch, put the backpack on.' 'Naw,' he said, 'I don't want the backpack on. It makes it harder landing, and I can't move around as well. I don't want the backpack.'

"I said, 'Put the backpack on, or by gosh, I'm not gonna take you up!' I just had a feeling, you know? He put the backpack on, and, by golly, when he jumped the first chute didn't open. It just snaked down and never did fill. And he pulled that backpack at the very last second. He landed hard, but he made it.

"When I landed he came up to me, white as a ghost. And he said, 'How did you know?' And I said, 'You just listen to me after this!' "

Roy Lumheim was a good friend through the years. During World War II he packed chutes for the Elementary Flying Training School at High River, then moved over to Foremost, Alberta.

In 1931, Lloyd Comba, a promoter, organized an aerial tour using 10 planes, called the Flying Frolics, with advance arrangements in towns all over Alberta and Saskatchewan. Boffa still has one of the old posters, with its "second coming" size of bold black type advertising the stars. Featured was Frank J. ("Wild Irish") Haddock, who had been the star parachute jumper in the movies *Hell's Angels, Wings* and *The Dawn Patrol.* He had made more than thirteen hundred parachute jumps at that time.

Ernie Boffa, "Famous Throughout the West For His Spectacular Flying," was partnered with "Wild Irish" Haddock. Haddock was from Montana, and used to jump from a balloon. He sat on a trapeze bar below the balloon on the ground, then when the balloon was released and floated aloft, he would hook himself to the chute bag tied to the trapeze bar, the same as the others did on the aircraft wing, and then he'd jump.

Haddock was never a pilot but Ernie recalls that he did everything else. He used to pull cars down the street with his teeth, as an ad. A new car would come out and the company would hire Frank to

FLYING FROLIC

And Parachute Performance!

See Formation Flying, Acrobats, Crazy Flying **THRILLS!**

Frank J. "Wild Irish" Haddock

Star Parachute Performer in "Hell's Angels," "Wings," and "The Dawn Patrol." Made Over 1300 Jumps.

Red Sherman, Cecil McNeal, Herb. Hopson, the Stunting Trio.

Passenger Carrying, $2 and $1
In Any Ship.

"Ernie" Boffa Famous Throughout the West for his Spectacular Flying, and Partner to Wild Irish Haddock.

Every Pilot Has Made Parachute Jumps

CHAMPION, WED. SEPT. 16

Grounds Admission, 25 Cents.

do this stunt, take the picture and run it in the ad saying, "It runs so easy, this guy can pull it with his teeth!"

In Montana, Haddock fitted a monkey with a small chute, and once up in the air, would drop the monkey, and thus get a pretty good idea of the wind drift. Then he'd go back up and do his own jump. Ernie explains that it was very important in those days to be able to judge the drift; you couldn't steer a chute then, as you can now. All you could do was slip it by spilling some air.

The "Stunting Trio" in the Frolics included Red Sherman, Cec McNeal and Herb Hobson. Red Sherman was a real scatter-brain pilot, Ernie recalls, the most unreliable guy in the world, but a very likable type. But Cec McNeal became Boffa's most trusted friend and partner for the next decade and more. They starved together and trusted each other with their lives on more than one occasion. McNeal began his flying career in 1928 and was an instructor at the Moosejaw Flying Club. He had logged more than 30,000 hours before he died in his CPAir jet in Tokyo, March 4, 1966, when he was chief pilot for the Pacific region.

The Flying Frolics did formation flying, aerobatics, parachute jumps and wingwalking, and took up passengers.

"I used to do this crazy flying," Ernie says. "A demonstration of what not to do. You gotta be good to get away with that, just like a comic skater or any other clown. They'd dress me up like an old woman, you know, and put me in an ambulance. Then they'd drive out on the field in front of the crowd, and I'd get out.

"They'd announce that I was going up for a ride to cure my deafness. (Flying was supposed to be good for your hearing troubles in those days!) I'd climb into the back cockpit of the plane. Then there'd be this pilot, helmet, goggles, breeches and boots, busy doing his stuff with switches, going around, turning the prop and all that, and then — by gosh! — the propeller would catch!

"He'd stand back surprised, I'd open the throttle a little and the airplane would start to move, and he'd step back out of the way, waving his arms. I'd open the throttle a little more and he'd start to run, trying to catch up and rescue me, the poor little old lady. Then I'd bounce her around a little more and finally pull her up into the air.

"Then I'd wobble around, up and down and around the field, while everybody in the crowd screamed in horror for that poor little old lady all alone up in that plane. Then if there was a dip in the field somewhere, I'd fly over and get in behind the hill and they'd lose sight of me. I'd maneuver around, flopping all over the sky, then come back in, heading right for the crowd. Everybody'd scatter! I'd finally come in, make a terrible landing, and bounce

Souvenir
Programme

Nᵒ 497

All Canadian Air Tours

Canadian Pilots and Canadian Ships
demonstrating old and new manouvers
in a big aerial circus

Price 25 cents

up and down awhile before I stopped. The pilot would run over, climb into the front cockpit, and taxi her in right in front of the crowd. Then they'd lift me out and drop me flat on the ground. I'd get up, squawking like mad, and chase them right off the field. That was the end of the act. It always went over very well.''

But his very first day with the Canadian Air Tour at Hanna, Alberta, didn't go over quite that well. Ernie had taken off with a young woman passenger on a routine flight, but knew there was something wrong when another plane took off immediately and flew alongside, the pilot pointing at the undercarriage of Boffa's Waco. Ernie leaned over and could see from the open cockpit that a strut had blown right out.

Without that strut to support the leading edge of the wing, the undercarriage would be completely lopsided on a landing and the wheel on the damaged side could smash into the wing. According to a news item in the Lethbridge paper at that time:

> After circling the field several times, Boffa finally made a perfect landing without injuring his passenger or plane in the slightest. T.L. Comba, Manager, and other members of the tour, as well as everyone who saw the incident, were loud in their praises of Boffa's feat.

Ernie says, "They called it a one-wheel landing. Well, you got to do the best you can but it's just common sense. You got to keep that side up as long as you can. You know one wheel is out there, you can't get rid of it. All hell breaks loose when the wheel hits that wing and the wing hits the ground. You know you're gonna be in trouble. But we were lucky that day."

The great Canadian Air Tour didn't actually survive very long in any case. The promoter didn't get around to doing much advance promoting and the pilots found themselves arriving in small prairie towns which weren't expecting them. They tried to get organized themselves, it dragged on a while longer, then fizzled out. There wasn't much frolic to their flying.

In the winters, when times were even tougher than in the summers, pilots worked at anything they could get. As a mechanic, Ernie never had trouble finding a job and could always fit in at a Lethbridge body shop. He worked at Hutton Electric too, where he wound generator armatures and became so expert he could do one in 40 minutes. He wound them by hand, dipped them in shellac, and then baked them.

Another pilot, Bob McCunn, later in the Royal Canadian Air Force, worked there at the same time as Ernie. And that brings

(Above) "Wild Irish" Haddock and Boffa, with Red Sherman spinning the prop of the WACO AQU, are about to thrill the crowd with their aerial antics.

(Right) Haddock and Boffa (arms folded) put on a casual "all in a day's work" act for the spectators. (Oliver, Calgary)

to mind the name of Deponcier, who flew into Lethbridge one day in a Waco taper-wing with a J-5 engine, selling ads to sponsor his trans-Canada flight. You could have your name or your company's name painted on the fuselage for five bucks, but Deponcier didn't get much action at that time. He suggested to Bob McCunn that they get a couple of girls and go out one night, and Bob agreed. Then Deponcier said they'd better take time to change before they picked up their dates. Bob said, "What do you mean, change? This is the only suit I have!" Ernie still chuckles about that.

Deponcier flew his plane into the snow at Ptarmigan Lake, up above Banff, Alberta. Ernie remembers that they had to take the aircraft apart to bring it down by river to the railroad, then into Lethbridge for repairs. That ended the dream of making a trans-Canada flight.

Ernie was still flying his Waco, and he had an interesting experience with the OX5.

"I'll tell you something about that OX5," he says. "They did about 1300 rpm and swung a great wooden club of a propeller. At 1250 they wouldn't perform very good, you had to have 1300 or better. Well, you could overhaul an OX5, put in new valves, rings, just about perfect, and you wouldn't get a single rpm more, just your 1300 again.

"So I got to wondering about this. I looked it over, measured the power stroke, and discovered that the thrust could be lengthened seven-sixteenths of an inch — almost half an inch — on the power stroke without interfering with the intake valve. You still got enough induction. It was an eight-cylinder engine. Well, when you take eight times that extra seven-sixteenths, you've got about three and a half inches of extra cylinder, see? That's just like having an extra cylinder with a three-and-a-half-inch stroke, eh?

"So that's what I did. I pulled the water pump off. The camshaft gear had very fine teeth, so I retarded the valves just enough to get this extra deal, put it back together, and — by God! — she picked up 100 rpm at the real business end.

"At that time, barnstorming in Canada, they wouldn't let you haul two passengers unless you could climb to 1,150 feet in three minutes. Now, this was a three-place airplane, with a wide cockpit in front. So I had 1400 rpm — you normally wouldn't get over 1300. So away we go. I climbed to beat hell and I made it.

"Well, nobody else with an OX5 was making it. There were a few others around, at Regina and places like that. Howard Ingram was inspector for the Department of Transport at that time. The other pilots told him, 'Well, gee, you can't climb like that in an OX5.' So he told them, 'Well, Boffa does, over at Lethbridge. His OX5 sure climbs.'

"He said he didn't know what I did to that engine, but maybe they should come over and find out. And a couple of them did come over and I showed them what to do — actually I did the work for them."

Ernie's theory was that Curtiss deliberately held down the power in that engine because the planes were used to teach student pilots in World War I Jennies.

"If you run them wide open all the time, you know what happens; they're not going to last. So I would say, just my own idea, they deliberately kept the power down."

Department of Transport inspectors had to be tough in those early days and they had plenty of time to take a long, hard look at everything about an airplane and a pilot. Jock Currie was an aircraft inspector who succeeded Inspector Luke, doing the aircraft checks during Howard Ingram's time as inspector of the fly boys.

"Jock didn't think twice about pulling your ticket if you tried to fool him. But he knew times were tough and he always gave us a chance to fix things up," Ernie remembers. "For example, there was this Stinson that used to break the tail ski when the load was heavy. So I tried to figure out a better way. I used a tail wheel inside a cup on the ski, a cap to hold it on with shock cords so it would give a little more. Worked fine.

"Jock came in one day. After he'd checked everything else in the hangar, I showed him the tail ski I'd altered. I'd learned it was the best policy to show him the strange stuff before he spotted it himself. So he said, 'What's this?' and had a close look at it. Then he straightened up. 'That's a helluva good deal, that ski thing,' he said. 'But don't let me catch you using it!' "

Ernie bought an Avian at Calgary, going cheap because one wing had been smashed in a crack-up. He set to work, repaired the wing, re-covered it with fabric and painted it. While he was away barn-storming, the DOT inspector came by and gave it a Certificate of Airworthiness for a completely re-covered aircraft! For this, Ernie gives credit to his own special mixture, a retarder-thinner mixed with the airplane dope.

"The trick was to work fast," he says. "Two men at once, on each side of the airplane, slapping it on until the fabric went soft. Then you let her dry, then apply the finish coat. Beautiful. It was like new fabric."

Charlie Tweed was by then the manager of the municipal field at Lethbridge and lived right there with his wife. He had a Monocoupe with a Genet Minor engine, an air-cooled radial five cylinder. These were smooth when new, Ernie recalls, but after heating up, the fins would bulge a bit. The cylinder became almost corrugated and would pump oil. Not a thing you could do about it.

"But Charlie Tweed did. He honed them out nice and smooth. He knew a good foundry man named Smerchuk, who had a workshop at home and could do aluminum castings. He honed the five cylinders out, cast the pistons, put them on a lathe and machined them to fit the honed-out cylinders. He experimented with the margin at extreme temperatures, and then he put it all back together again. Those cylinders worked fine.

"But somebody squealed to Jock Currie, who had to come then and inspect them. He marched in one day and said, 'Let's see these back yard pistons.' And, of course, he had to condemn them according to the rule book, and Charlie had to get rid of that engine."

Aviation was young and so were the aviators when, in 1931, almost all the pilots of Calgary got together for a photo. There were, back row, left to right: Gil McClaren, Charlie Tweed, Kendall, "Smitty" Smith, Lionel Vines (he was killed while flying with Yukon Southern at Carcross), Sandy Sangath (one of the first pilots with Trans-Canada Airlines), Joe Patton (he did the first parachute jump at Lethbridge), Cec McNeal, Kirkham (he went into the RCAF), Homer Carr, Herbie Hobson (retired, much later, from Trans-Canada Airlines), Bruce Waddell (he was the airport manager).
In the front row: Chet Kullberg, Lloyd Comba (promoter of the Flying Circus), Freddy McCall (who shot down 37 enemy planes during World War I), Howard Ingram (first aviation inspector based in Regina), Frank Haddock, Ernie Boffa, Red Sherman, Joe Irwin, name unknown (a non-pilot from Calgary's radio station), and Captain F.R. McCall (Canada's No. 1 flying ace in World War I, DSO, MC, DFC and Bar, one of the original pilots with Great Western Airways). Not here, presumably flying when the photo was made, is Capt. "Jock" Palmer (DFC and Bar, MM and, according to Boffa, one of the greatest).

Charlie Tweed was killed at Juneau, Alaska, flying for Yukon Southern just before World War II, but not before his young son, Sandy, soloed in the Monocoupe at the age of 11. All the Lethbridge pilots had a special party for him, and all went dressed as kids. Joe Irwin and Ernie Boffa, good friends of Charlie and Lil Tweed, saw Sandy through to his pilot's license. Later Sandy turned up as a crewman for Ernie in the Northwest Territories. He went on with CPAir to become a captain on 747s, before taking early retirement, and in 1979 was enjoying being chief pilot for his son Bill Tweed's company, Simpson Air, at Fort Nelson and Fort Simpson.

40

PARTNERS IN POVERTY

One of the jobs that helped pay the bills at Lethbridge for a while was Ernie's contract to do the flying for an oil company named Del Bonita. Ernie used his Puss Moth. He had sold the Waco and bought an American Eagle from Art Craig in Flaxcomb. It was a rare bird; only a few were ever made. Then he traded it to Muncaster for the Moth. It was a good plane for the oil company job, equipped with skis during the winter season when all the haul roads were blocked by snow.

Newspaper headlines of the day proclaimed "Airplane Keeps Wildcat Well Going at Del Bonita in Southwestern Alberta," and the story in the Great Falls paper explained:

> An airplane has been placed in service to keep a wildcat well working amid sub-zero temperatures and 18 inches of snow on Del Bonita structure in southern Alberta, a short distance north of the Montana line. An account of the unusual oil well operation was brought to Great Falls this week by Warren Hough, acid well treater, who has been snowbound at the Del Bonita camp for two weeks, until the airplane was chartered by the owners of the well, the Terminal Oil Company.
>
> A group of Californians, generally regarded as "tenderfeet" in the he-man country to the north, are carrying on this operation, said to be the only active well in the province of Alberta. Except for the airplane, it would be virtually impossible for them to continue, for the roads are blocked by high drifts, in addition to the 18 inches on the level.
>
> Meantime, S. Myron Zandmer, President of Terminal Oil, had succeeded in getting word out to Lethbridge, to hire Ernest Boffa, veteran pilot, to fly out to Del Bonita. The pilot made a safe landing near the rig, and Zandmer chartered the plane to carry passengers and supplies. It is possible to carry only a light load because of the difficulty of getting off the ground.

That a new oil field has been opened by this Del Bonita strike is generally accepted in the industry, irrespective of the outcome of the present test. It is 5,000-foot drilling, and wells will have to do 100 barrels or better to be commercial, observers say.

Ernie grins when he reads that old clipping, especially the bit about "light loads." One of the things he hauled for Del Bonita was a five-hundred-pound drilling jar. The six-foot-long steel jar was wired into the belly of the Moth, fastened to the tail skid at the Lethbridge runway, and flown to the drill site at Del Bonita.

"And, by golly, it worked!" He made the papers again with that. The hairiest experience on that oil well assignment that he can recall was caused by a whiteout, something every northern pilot dreads.

Too big to go inside? Lash it on outside and Captain Boffa would fly it. He knew precisely what each plane could haul.

Pat Adams, the chief driller at Del Bonita, wanted to get some equipment at the company's second well at Twin River, so he hopped into the Moth with Boffa. They took off late one winter afternoon in a dull overcast. By the time they had picked up the parts and were ready to head for home, they were into ice fog as soon as they got higher than the low hills around them. The plane was icing up, so Ernie knew he had to land. Just as a white slope loomed up in front of him, Boffa cut the throttle and landed uphill on that slope, slid over the top and down the other side, and to a stop halfway up the next slope.

"It was like a nightmare," Ernie says. "In half an hour I couldn't see from one wingtip to another. So we took the compass out of the plane and started walking in the cold. We finally reached a road, then found a lane to a farmhouse, and got a place to sleep for the rest of the night. We had walked eight miles and had some frostbite to show for it.

"In the morning the farmer got out his wooden sledge, harnessed up one of his horses, and we loaded a stove, pipes, canvas and tools on that thing and went looking for the airplane. The horse pulled that stuff for miles before we finally located the Moth. We put a canvas tent over the engine, warmed her up with the stove, and, by golly, she turned over. We thanked the farmer — and the horse — and took off for Del Bonita again."

That well came in with gas, Ernie recalls.

"You could hear the rumbling down in the hole, and I got the hell out of there fast! The pressure was so great it pushed the swab right up to the top and dislodged the Christmas tree — then it all froze. The crew got a steam outfit and thawed her out, but she went right through the boards and put the foreman's eye out with a piece of gravel, just like a bullet out of a gun."

While he was flying the Moth for Del Bonita, Ernie's Avian was being flown by pilot Craig of Kindersley. And after the oil rig charter ended, Ernie was up at Lesser Slave Lake, hauling fish in the Puss Moth. He was finishing a contract pilot W.F.S. Luck couldn't carry out because his Boeing biplane had been destroyed by fire. That was the same plane used by Canadian Airways for air-mail service at Lethbridge, then flown to Vancouver by H. Hollick-Kenyon, who was later lost in the Antarctic.

There were other flying jobs more enjoyable than hauling fish. Occasionally a sports fan in Lethbridge would charter Boffa and his Moth to take the two of them to see a hockey game in Calgary on a Saturday night. If it was a good game they'd stay over to see the return engagement Monday night. Charlie Tweed was doing the same and, in winter flying conditions, sometimes had trouble getting the businessman home again.

One outing they enjoyed together was when Boffa and Tweed were engaged to fly to Calgary and carry members of the Calgary Ski Club up near Banff for ski races. They landed on wheels at Lake Chestermere, changed to skis, and flew up to Ptarmigan Lake. But things didn't work out as planned. Ptarmigan Lake, where the skiers were going to land, then ski three miles to Skoki Lake where the races were being held, is up over seventy-four hundred feet altitude. When the planes got there they found poor visibility and a low ceiling; in fact, the lake was in the clouds that day.

President A.N. Carscallen of the Calgary Ski Club was

disappointed, but agreed with the pilot that "Them clouds is full of rocks." Carscallen was satisfied to return safely to home base.

One other family business highlight during the Lethbridge days, which must be mentioned, was The Pantry.

One hungry winter Ernie joined up with Mousie Marks to open a restaurant. Mousie got a few bucks from his father and Ernie worked out his partnership in the venture by building all the booths, stools and furnishings for the place. In the spring of 1932 Boffa sold Marks his interest and went back to flying.

That autumn, when flying slowed down again, Ernie and Nettie bought Marks out and took over the operation of The Pantry themselves. Nettie's sister Peggy and brother Andrew all pitched in and helped whenever they could, and Ernie had Roy Lumheim do the butchering. Everybody helped with the dishes. The display ad they ran in the *Lethbridge Herald* gives some idea of their optimistic imagination, if not experience in the restaurant business!

The cook was pretty good, Ernie remembers, but, as proprietor, he refused to settle for anything but the best. He would taste her products out in the kitchen, and sometimes throw them into the garbage.

"Then she'd start to cry," Ernie says. "But it worked, and we

44

Flying the open-cockpit Fox Moth was "making money the hard way." Here the Moth off-loads on Emma Lake, Saskatchewan.

kept the standards high at The Pantry. The food was so good they used to stand in line to get in, even during the dirty thirties.''

The flying fraternity soon knew that any local pilot could eat at The Pantry free of charge. But it was also an unwritten law that he would peel a few potatoes to help out. Even Grant McConachie took advantage of that system once.

One night, when E.J.B. himself was spelling the cook in the kitchen, an order came out for a T-bone steak. So Ernie took care of that order personally, steak being as rare as rubies. He made sure the plate was good and hot, and all the trimmings were in place, then sent it in to this special customer — only to learn it was for fellow pilot Cec McNeal, who was just as broke as the rest of them! Cec was given plenty of time to work that off.

Charlie and Lil Tweed used to come in from the airport every weekend to help out, and The Pantry became a social center for pilots and their families that winter. Looking back now, Nettie and Ernie remember a lot of good times when they had fun, working hard and enjoying life, not knowing what a tough time they were going through!

In the spring, when flying provided work again, they sold The Pantry to their cook. Ernie says she started cutting corners, and not long afterward went out of business. But she probably didn't get as much volunteer help as the Boffas had.

In 1932, Cec McNeal and Ernie teamed up.

"We were going to go 50/50 on everything, you know, and we pooled everything we had, airplanes, equipment and so on. Well, just to show you how tough things were, Cec had a pair of air-wheels, those old soft doughnut things, big, low-pressure tires. After a few years they began to get cracked. Finally, one of those tires gave way, after running into gopher holes and the odd rock and so on for so long.

"So he patched it with a piece of soft leather and a leather shoe lace, poked holes, and sewed the lace through, and it kept him flying. The pressure was so low anyway, it didn't matter a great deal. But he didn't want to run into his brother-in-law, who was Inspector Howard Ingram, because Ingram, in all fairness, would have been tougher on Cec than on the rest of us, just because of his being his wife's brother!

"Cec had a Gypsy Moth, and the engine had thrown a rod just before he got it. To show you how scarce money was in those days, they had actually patched the crankcase. There was a big patch on it, with bolts all around a steel plate. And that was just the beginning!

"In those days we thought the spark plugs that came with the airplane should pretty well last the life of the plane. They were KLG plugs, mica plugs, made up of little rings of mica squeezed up in the insulator. These things would get oil-soaked and then they would miss. McNeal had these KLGs — they looked pretty old. I guess they had come with the aircraft.

"When we were out barnstorming at night we used to go into the nearest town and stay most of the time with the Chinaman. In every small town the Chinaman had rooms over his restaurant, and we ate there as well. So we used to put Cec's spark plugs on the stove in the kitchen and bake them overnight, bake the oil out of them every chance we'd get. In the morning, we'd tighten up the plugs, set them, gap them, put the plugs in the airplane and get ready to start the day.

"Roy Lumheim, our parachute jumper, and I would watch him. Cec would adjust the throttle, switch off, and he'd suck it in, go back and crank the throttle and turn the switch on, and then go up forward, taking his time, nice and easy like. And he'd pull the prop down and if it didn't catch the first time he'd look at it and he'd say, 'Well.'

"He'd pull it a second time, and if it didn't start, he'd say, 'Well, for goodness sake.' He'd go back and forth, maybe half a dozen times, through this routine before the thing would start. But he never lost his temper.

"One thing I'd like to say about McNeal — he never cussed — never used a cuss word. He was the pleasantest guy you ever traveled with, you know. A real nice guy. He never ran anybody down. I liked him."

There certainly had to be that kind of mutual admiration to get the partners through some of their hard times together.

Before they started out on that particular barnstorming trip, Ernie recalls, Cec had wintered at a little town near Moosejaw, fixing up this Gypsy Moth to fly again. He needed a propeller, so he built one.

"He did a good job, laminated it and everthing," says Boffa. "It looked exactly like one you'd buy from de Havilland. But he had to avoid Howard Ingram, you know, because of the prop, the patch on the crankcase, and all that sort of thing.

"One day at Brooks, Alberta, we were getting ready for a big sports day crowd, and in the morning we gassed up and were raring to go. Cec was inspecting the Waco, and he grabbed a strut and gave it a shake — and it bent in his hand! His face went white. We didn't know what to do. So we took out the strut and drove into town to the local blacksmith and got a buggy wheel spoke there. I shaved the end down to the same shape as the inside of the strut and we shoved her in, and away we went. It didn't seem to make any difference."

Experimenting with aircraft was part of the fun for Boffa. It was always a challenge to him, to be faced with an impossible load, or to contrive a solution to a new problem.

One day in the summer of 1934 he was flying a passenger named Lynn Fairbairn, a Lethbridge lawyer and World War I pilot, to Medicine Hat on business.

"We just got nicely airborne and then, just over the government's Experimental Farm, the gas shut off, the valve disconnected, and she quit cold on me. We weren't very high, so I did a maybe less-than-90° turn and landed right in a plowed field. Got away with it.

"So, of course, everybody came running out. We fixed the valve, then they helped us taxi her over to a smoother field to take off. While all this was going on, these guys were talking about the grasshoppers. It was a bad year, and they were saying, 'Why couldn't we spray the grasshopper bait from the air?'

"So this gave me an idea. I went to see a guy I knew at the North Lethbridge garage. He was a real handy craftsman; he could make anything if he thought it was a good idea. So we built this thing to go under this old Waco biplane I was using. It hung on the plane's belly, just as an experiment to see how it worked, and it worked pretty good. We had this belt and a conveyor to drag the stuff off. The mix of molasses and sawdust and arsenic wouldn't run like a liquid; you had to shake it off.

"So in the meantime, I got a hold of this American Eagle, a little bigger, a closed-in, four-place job. And we cut a hole in the roof

McConachie's Ford Trimotor, used for hauling fish in winter, was easily converted for spreading grasshopper bait.

and loaded the grasshopper bait from there, and it worked fine. I did two or three private jobs for farmers.

"Then Grant McConachie heard about this and came down and looked it over. He thought it looked pretty good. He had a Ford Trimotor, used mostly for hauling fish in winter, and he had nothing much for it to do in the summer. We looked over the Trimotor, and had to get a special O.K. from the Department of Transport to cut a slit in the belly. We got a temporary O.K. so long as we plugged it up again when the plane reverted to normal flying operations. So we were all set.

"We figured we could charge 10¢ an acre to spread the grasshopper bait from the air. The farmers were using up to 30 pounds per acre, spreading it by hand, and we had it down to 3 pounds per acre from the air. So we could save the government money by doing the job for a lousy 10¢ per acre. Anyway we told the government people we were all set, and we could cover the shoulders and ditches right to the edge of the field in the same pass as we went over the fields. A real good deal for them.

"Well, we never got an answer — not until the following year, by which time I was up in Prince Albert. They said they had $10,000 approved in their departmental budget for us to come down and experiment at the farm with the equipment, but hell, we'd already done all the experimenting! We wanted to do the spraying. That's the way the government always operates — too late. They could have said, come down and do some spreading, but no, it was just experimenting. Well, neither of us did anything more about it. But I think that was the first experimental spraying from the air in the Canadian west.

"Joe Irwin of Canadian Airways, and a guy named Christensen, were building a sort of canvas hopper bag. Their prop agitated the bag and spilled the stuff out. But they didn't get any action out of the government either.''

In 1935, McNeal had joined the flying staff of M and C Air Services in northern Saskatchewan, and Boffa followed him the next year. Mason, the ''M,'' had been in the British Army Air Force, before the Royal Flying Corps, in World War I. The ''C'' was Angus Campbell, a Saskatchewan man described by Ernie Boffa as ''a most ingenious guy'' with a great experimental and mechanical ability. They used a Stinson, Fox Moth and Fairchild. Their greatest proportion of business, by far, was hauling fish and fishermen.

Ernie was impressed by Campbell, and he participated in the design and making of the first pneumatic ski pedestal, later used throughout the country.

''I tested the very first one,'' Ernie remembers. ''He only made one at first, which just shows you how chintzy things were in the thirties. It was too expensive to make two if they weren't going to work! He was a real good man, Angus Campbell, a good pilot and all-round handyman, but very careful with his cash!

''Angus used to sit around and wait for a tail wind when we weren't too busy. In northern Saskatchewan they called it an 'M and C' wind. I remember going up to Buffalo Narrows on the sched run, and bedding down in the shack at night, and old Tom Peterson would wake me up and say, 'Hey, Ernie, you better get going, you've got an M and C wind.' ''

Working for M and C, Boffa was paid $135 per month and no expense money. But in those days, on that pay, he could afford to bring Nettie and baby daughter Kay up to Big River with him. They stayed in the hotel there, in first-class style.

Most of Ernie's flying was with the commercial fishermen. All winter they set nets, hauled fish out of the freezing water, brought them by horse-drawn sleighs over lake ice to the nearest road, then shipped them by rail to southern Canada. They used teams of horses and sleighs, led by a loaded wagon, with a snowplow attached. The rest all followed in its track.

The planes flew low, riding back and forth, bringing supplies for both men and horses.

''That was really making money the hard way,'' says Ernie today, ''flying northern Saskatchewan winters in an open-cockpit Fox Moth. We contrived our own arctic flying gear. The Indian women around there were pretty handy at sewing and we got them to make us duffle coats and caribou socks, worn with the fur inside, then over that we'd put on mukluks with felt insoles. They made us warm parkas and we even used face masks.''

Remembering those cold winter flights, Ernie recalls with affection an Icelandic woman, Mrs. Skivik, who, with her husband, ran a stopping place at Dore Lake, patronized by the drivers and their teams. They stopped overnight in a bunkhouse there.

"She was the greatest cook in the world!" Boffa declares, more than 40 years later. "You'd sit down on the ice in that Fox Moth, half-frozen, and she'd run out with a bag of hot fish cakes. Oh, boy! You never tasted anything as good in your life. Your hands would be so stiff and cold you could hardly get the food into your mouth. Then came some scalding, strong coffee. She was a very kind woman and her husband was a real nice, hard-working guy."

Lowell Dunsmore was flying for M and C at that time too, and the Fox Moth gave him a lot of trouble. In the spring of 1937, M and C got the government Natural Resources contract, and one day soon after, a radiogram was delivered to the Prince Albert office from the Natural Resources station farther north. The message read, "Please send us a new plane. This one is no good." Signed Fred Redhead, Dunsmore's nickname.

M and C had a Fairchild which Ernie flew, G-CARA. It had been built for Duke Schiller, a famous American pilot of those days, and had been specially welded for extra tanks in preparation for his attempt at a transatlantic crossing. Ernie says it was lucky he didn't try it — he would never have got off the ground in that plane. Besides, Lindbergh beat him to it. Nobody liked that Fairchild, and Angus Campbell finally cracked up in her.

There's another part to that story about the ski pedestal. Campbell left a gap between the shaft and the pedestal, and cut strips of thick rubber inner tubes to make one big, long rubber band. Then he wrapped that around the axle and put the pedestal on, put the cap on and the washers — then let the elastic go. Having the rubber there made it very flexible and it was great for side movement in cold weather.

Ernie was flying gunnysacks of fresh fish to Clear Lake, for the tractor train to haul out to Big River, and he came steaming in for a landing one cold day. The rubber gripped the axle and sheared the bolt and away went the ski.

"Down goes the wing," Ernie recalls, "but it didn't quite scrape the ice. The flange of the ski apparatus cut the ice like a saw. The load of fish behind me kept the tail down, so we groundlooped. No damage. We unloaded, replaced the bolt, flew her home."

The Company of Adventurers (the Hudson's Bay Company) started an outpost at Cree Lake, on the route from Patuanac, with a portage at Pine River. They built skiffs and pulled the loads as far as they could go, up to Jackpine Flats, where it was very sandy,

with lots of wild blueberries. Then there was a portage of a couple of miles, after which the boats could get back into the chain of lakes leading to Cree Lake.

"They wanted a car there to haul stuff across the portage," Ernie says. "They bought a Ford in Prince Albert, and sent it up on a scow to Isle La Crosse and Patuanac, where the Churchill River begins. Then they took it apart, put the parts on the skiffs, and hauled them to the portage. Then I flew up, put the Ford together (child's play for the mechanic who built the *Dreadnought!*) and attached a trailer to it.

"So all they had to do then was bring in the skiffs, unload them onto the trailer, the Ford would haul it across the two-mile portage,

Boffa (center) in his Puss Moth and Charlie Tweed in his Monocoupe, flying Calgary skiers to races in Banff, sat down on Chestermere Lake to change from wheels to skis.

then the loads went back on the water. That was the beginning of shipping regular supplies to Cree Lake for the HBC.''

Boffa and McNeal began talking about leaving M and C and running their own air service. In the spring of 1937 Cec quit, and they bought a Stinson from Tommy Lamb, a well-known operator in northern Manitoba at that time.

"I was in it with him," Ernie says, "but he quit first. We organized it together and I was to join him later. I had promised to fly for Canadian Airways, so I kept my promise. And after flying for a salary all summer, I actually quit at freezeup and we all went to Big River. Now that was a real starvation deal! We never saw a dime. We were hauling fish all winter and the fishermen would pay you with an order on next year's fish! We had barely enough cash to pay for the gasoline.

"Our schedule was supposed to run up to Peter Pond Lake, Isle La Crosse and Buffalo Narrows once a week. But if we didn't have a load we'd just delay the trip. It was pretty skinny up there, you know. Fish were selling for three cents a pound, on the ice. There was just no money. So heck, we weren't going to fly up there unless we had a load.

"Anyway, our schedule was posted at Buffalo Narrows, and after a while they saw the light. They knew we weren't going to be there right on the dot. So at the post office, they put up another sign beside our schedule. It read: 'McNeal Air Service. Monday or Tuesday for sure; Wednesday or Thursday at least; if we're not here Friday or Saturday, don't expect us until next week!' Boy, that was just about it, too.

"In Big River, we had our own outfit using the Stinson we bought from Lamb. Jules Marion was seeking reelection as Liberal candidate against Bill Windrom, who was running as an Independent in Meadow Lake. McNeal flew Jules up to do some electioneering at Goldfields, and on the way home the gas line broke. Gas squirted all over the Stinson's exhaust pipe and it caught fire.

"Cec shut off the gas, but by this time the plane's belly was on fire. The flames were burning toward the back, so Cec goes into a sideslip until he gets close to the ground, and he still has control. There was a lake ahead of him, so he just pancaked into that lake, and splash! The water put the fire out.

"Cec fixed the gas line. They took off and flew into Big River with the fuselage all burned to bits and flapping in rags, the bottom burned right out — but still flying.

"You learn some lessons the hard way. We were using the Fox Moth, a three-place wooden aircraft with a closed cabin and open front cockpit for the pilot. One of our customers, Muskeg Mary, had a goat and wanted another pair flown up to her place from Big River. So we tied those two animals in the cabin and flew them up to her. Well, they were pretty scared, of course, and I hate to tell you what they did to that cabin and its wooden floor! Moral: *Never fly a goat!* No matter how hard we scrubbed and cleaned the plane, the stink was there for months."

Pilots who survived soon learned every trick in the trade.

"Sometimes you'd get into a tough spot — maybe land in a very small lake, on floats. You had to take a chance to get out again. So you'd adjust the propeller pitch and get two or three hundred

54

more rpm just when you needed them, then change it back later. Nobody ever mentioned it.

"Another little trick was to adjust the aileron droop, to give the effect of flap at the end of the wing. It gave you just that little bit of extra that you needed at times. One day in the late summer of 1937, flying for Canadian Airways, I was hauling a field team of the Geological Survey of Canada from one lake to another, using the Bellanca Skyrocket. It was a real dog. On takeoff, when loaded, you couldn't get more than 75 or 80 — the same speed to land or to climb! That particular day, the lake was just too small for a normal takeoff run, so I changed the pitch, dropped the ailerons, and took off in a circling turn, round and round inside the hills until we had enough height to get over. We made it all right.

"One of the survey boys was impressed, I guess. Anyway, he named the lake after me on the mapping sheets they were putting together north of Isle La Crosse, and sent the blueprints in to officials in Ottawa. I never heard any more about it until recently, when old friends from northern Saskatchewan were down here in Los Angeles for a visit and told me my name has been on that lake for years."

On another trip in the fall of '37, that Bellanca was on the sched run from Prince Albert to Goldfields, via Fond du Lac and Stoney Rapids, overnighting at Isle La Crosse.

"We had the airplane facing into shore. It was quite calm and nothing to worry about. We had a heavy load of meat for Jimmy Mason at Viola Lake and liquor for Goldfields. In the morning we came out and found the tail on the bottom and icicles hanging from the dock.

The J6 Wright engine in the Bellanca Pacemaker later "swallowed" its last valve and crashed in the Bush. (Courtesy CPAir)

55

"There was no way out. I had to wade into that icy water and pull up the tail and pump the water out of the floats. Cold? I've never been so cold and wet in all my life, before or since!"

That same Bellanca, a Pacemaker with a J6 Wright (Boffa calls it the world's worst engine), used to swallow valves. If you were fast enough to land and get her — you pulled the cylinder off, took the broken valve out, took the push rod out and flew home on eight cylinders. After that happened three times, Boffa started carrying an extra cylinder.

"I complained a lot about that engine, and finally talked Sears, the maintenance super for Canadian Airways, into doing something about it. He sent another J6 E Series engine, with 300-310 horsepower, nine cylinders — said it was supposed to be better."

Ernie tested the new engine in Prince Albert, after he had installed it in the Bellanca. He heard rattling inside and knew it wasn't right; it sounded like a blower clutch. He wrote on the test report, "Clutch defective."

"No, no," said Sears, "nothing wrong."

So E.J.B. flew it for the rest of the season, then turned it over to pilot North Saule. Saule kept it at Goldfields. After freezeup, Al Parker was flying her, and, at a lake north of Isle La Crosse, crashed her into the Bush. So Ernie was right.

North Saule later flew for CPAir, and was captain of a Comet jetliner flying from Great Britain to Australia in 1953, when he was killed, with the rest of the aircrew, in Karachi during a takeoff crash. From Athabaska, North Saule was a pilot at 17 years of age, and at 20 was flying for Mackenzie Air Services, piloting a Junkers to Aklavik. He joined CPAir in 1942, and was chief pilot for overseas service at the time of his death.

McNeal and Boffa hit economic rock-bottom in 1938, but still hung tough together. One more year and they would have made it, Ernie says now. Once the war started, the price of fish went up like a rocket.

"We hung together until September 1939, when World War II started," Ernie says. "Then Cec left to fly for Canadian Airways, and later for CPAir. We sold the business back to M and C, with an understanding that I would stay and fly for them for at least a year. So that's why I couldn't get in at the beginning of the war, when the gravy was being handed out to experienced pilots. I had promised to stay until spring, and I stayed.

"So when I finally got down there to join up, I got the work but not the gravy. But anyway, I don't regret it. I figure everybody has to do something for the country, and I did my share."

6

AIR FORCE DAYS

In the summer of 1940 Ernie Boffa went to Saskatoon to join the Royal Canadian Air Force. He had to take a test at the University of Saskatchewan to prove he had the educational equivalent of grade eight. Once again, his lack of formal schooling was a handicap.

"I had to fight to get into the air force," Ernie says. "And, of course, my place of birth being Italy didn't help matters much. The medical examiner when I went through was Dr. McPhail from Kindersley, whom I knew real well. I had flown him on numerous occasions. So when my eyes were examined and found a little on the weak side, he told the eye man to pass me regardless. Of course, they caught up with me later on at Prince Albert and prescribed glasses — which I never wore."

Officially sworn into the Royal Canadian Air Force in August, Boffa was soon checked out on all the aircraft available and joined the staff at No. 6 Elementary Flying Training School at Prince Albert, Saskatchewan, as an instructor in September 1940. He lived off the base with Nettie, daughter Kay, and baby Joan, who was born there. He was there until February 1943, flying nothing much but Tiger Moths and training candidates for air crew.

During the first few months at the school, the air force asked for volunteers for overseas service. Ernie and another instructor named Hall volunteered immediately, and were accepted. But they were never called, despite their frequent inquiries; a long time later Ernie discovered the whole thing had been pigeon-holed in an official desk somewhere and forgotten. Quite a number of instructors at the flying schools across Canada were affected by that official faux pas.

Ernie Boffa, for example, despite having voluntarily enlisted, despite having volunteered for active service overseas, despite flying every day of his service and putting in twenty six hundred hours of flying instruction on duty, never got past the temporary rank of sergeant-instructor, which he considered the equivalent of a glorified "acey-deucey," AC/2 (aircraftsman second class) in the RCAF. The instructors serving at the Elementary Flying Training schools of that period did not wear RCAF uniforms, nor were they given "wings," even though in Boffa's case his official capacity was assistant chief flying instructor.

They had 12 instructors to start with, but conditions were changing. The initial need had been to provide instant pilots to bolster up the British forces during the ferocious aerial Battle of Britain, but the emphasis changed as the war continued.

"Before I was discharged they had so many pilots they didn't know what to do with them," Ernie remembers. "They were sending these guys back to get more hours and making instructors out of them. Some of us older guys had the option of discharge if we wanted, because it didn't pay the air force to send us to service school for training and all that military stuff. At one time we had more than 30 instructors on our list.

"We had good men in our flight. Our line was always at the top of the school. There were Pringle, Abe Dyke [whose brother flew for Eldorado], Red Francis, Sabinsky — all volunteered for overseas.

"Our school used to get the efficiency awards among the EFTS's, and we had no accidents. Later, when the air force took over officially, things changed. They went strictly by the book. I used to throw the book away; I taught the guys every safety method and all the flying tricks I had learned the hard way."

Ernie's students certainly got a lot of extras. They flew on skis in Saskatchewan for winter training. He would finish them early on the regular instruction, then take them out where there was a big, empty field (there are plenty of those in Saskatchewan!), and set up a little competition. There'd be a case of beer for the best forced landing, the best spot landing. He made the scary stuff into a game. That way, Ernie's students learned to make decisions for themselves in a moment of crisis.

Letters came back to their instructor after his boys went on for further training. One, from Debert, Nova Scotia, is typical. "Have covered quite a bit of ground since we were up together that last day in the snow, when you were doing your best to show me how to set a Moth down beside a stick in the field. Would like to try it again, for the beers. Think I could run you a close second now!

"One of my WAGs [wireless air gunner] and I were talking and he mentioned Prince Albert EFTS and come to find out, he was washed out of a class or two before ours and you were his instructor. It sure is a coincidence that we should be crewed up together and this crew is supposed to stick together permanently. He is a P/O [pilot officer] and seems to be right up on the bit, which means a lot when it comes to radio these days.

58

"Have finally ended up here to get the final polish on our flying, which was getting a little rusty. Got away solo in eight hours, second in the class, and like the Hudsons fine, lots of poop. Getting along fine, and hope you are the same . . ."

Wash out. That was a dirty word at any EFTS.

"I used to hate to see a kid wash out, especially if it was just a matter of poor instruction," Ernie says. "I remember this one guy, he had remustered from ground crew. Now that's a guy you sure don't want to wash out. But he just could not cut it. He could not land that airplane. And I knew what was wrong with him; he was looking too close — he was looking at the ground. You got to look far enough ahead so you can see the ground, sure, but you should also see the horizon and the attitude of your plane's nose, all at the same time.

"So I didn't know what to do with this guy. Two or three instructors tried to help him. We used to get four or five hours' flying per month for instrument time, or whatever, for our own flying, and we chiseled an hour here and there to work with him. They gave me their extra time. I'd donate it to a student having some trouble, and not show it in his logbook. What the hell, the idea was to get them through. I finally got mad at this guy and said, 'You're not looking at the right place when you land!'

"So I got this bright idea. I went over to the shop. I got this welding rod and made a circle, a ring, and fastened it on the airplane. Then we went out on the field and I put out one of those markers, at just the distance you should be looking ahead on a landing. I sat him in the airplane and had him tell me when he saw that thing right in the middle. 'O.K.,' he told me when he saw it in the middle of the ring. We adjusted the ring. Then I told him, 'Don't you dare look anywhere else but through that ring when you come in to land.' And, by gosh, that did it. Half a dozen landings and he had it! That was the missing link!"

How many young men did Boffa teach to fly at No. 6 EFTS? Well, there was a new course starting every three weeks. Each instructor had three of those junior students, plus three seniors from the previous course for a six-week total. So, six at a time, week after week after week, there must have been several hundred pilot officers instructed by E.J.B. Near the end of his service with the air force, Ernie was busy with other things as well, checking finals, checking wash outs, and handling administrative paperwork.

As might be expected, he had his own methods.

"I used to take my group up right away, as soon as they unpacked. I'd look them over, then pick the brightest guy and solo him on his second day, get him on his own a little bit. Then the next day I'd solo the second best, and then the third. They had to have a minimum of 8 hours' instruction — later this requirement was upped to 10 — but my idea was to do it fast, give the bright ones a chance to show the way.

"One thing I could never get through to the air force types was that if you let a student spend time doing the circuit of the whole field between practice landings, you've wasted a whole lot of valuable time. So I used to take my students away from the airport to a forced-landing field we had close by, a good, big stubble field. I'd line her up and show them one approach, land, and take off; just touch and go. Then I'd whip her around, real fast, line her up, turn over to the student and we'd come in, bounce, give her the gun, learn how to handle the torque, and take off again. That way I could give them 15 or 20 landings in an hour, instead of the usual 3 or 4 circuits of the whole airport. Boy! Those fellows would come back to the airport and it was just a piece of cake after that open field practice!"

Ernie used a little home-grown psychology on them, as well. "You know, if you want a guy to do a really good job of something, all you've got to do is give him something tougher than that, and, by gosh, the first job looks easier when you go to work on it. After they had about five hours' solo, I used to tell them, 'There's no point in having you practice climbing up out of the airport, you know how to do that, and how to make your first turn, so we might as well put the hood up.' And I had them doing instrument flying practically as soon as they soloed.

"And you know what that did? It smoothed out their flying, took off the rough edges, and they were really smooth. Mind you, I just gave them enough to get used to watching that level on climb and turn, then off came the hood and away they'd go. After that, they'd talk to the others, and, of course, brag a little bit, you know. 'This looking outside the plane is nothing — wait until you get under the hood!' Boy, they loved it."

At first, working as an air force instructor was very much like being a civilian. Then, in the fall and winter of 1942-43, when the RCAF took over operation of the schools, the instructors were issued sergeants' uniforms.

"Suddenly, we really had to toe the mark," says Ernie. "Well, I didn't get along too well with the commanding officer. I knew his background from my flying days in Calgary, and he was afraid I'd tell someone that he didn't really have all that experience. Of course I never did, but he always tried to make it miserable for me anyway.

"So one day they put one of these young guys with the white

arm band [officer in training] in charge as orderly officer, and I'm on DRO [Daily Routine Orders] as orderly sergeant. So you know what I did? I went home and I stayed there.

"Next day, when I came to work, they called me up to the adjutant's office to explain why I didn't show on DRO. I told him straight, he'd never get me to do that. When he asked why I told him. To start with, I'd never had a minute's drill instruction, so I didn't know how to conduct myself properly. And I would not wear the king's uniform — nor the queen's for that matter — unless I could do it properly, I told him. So I said, 'You can hang me, shoot me, or courtmartial me, do anything you like, I'm not going to do it.' And, by gosh, I got away with it.

"They knew my record as an instructor, down at Western Command Headquarters, and I got a very nice letter from Wing Commander [later group captain] Bonham Carter.

"Anyway, I left in February 1943 and ferried a Fairchild to Edmonton for M and C, who were working for the Canol Pipeline project by then. Bob Randall was on loan to them from CPAir, in charge of the flying for the Canol, and he suggested I join them. So I talked to McConachie and he said he'd like to have me go to Yellowknife and fly the run from there to Great Bear Lake.

"It was a high priority deal. CPAir had got two Lockheed Lodestars on the strength of servicing the vitally important uranium mine at Eldorado, on Great Bear. It looked just fine to me, but I had to go through the Wartime Selective Board office at Edmonton.

"So I got to Selective Service and I said, 'I want to fly for CPAir.' And this guy says, 'You can't go to work for CPAir. First of all, there's the Canol Project, then there's Leigh Brintnell's aircraft repair outfit here overhauling planes, and they need a test pilot.'

"So I got mad. And I said, 'What the hell do you mean, I can't go to work for CPAir? What have you done in this war? Have you been in the service?' He said no. 'Well,' I said, 'you mean to tell me that after all this time doing my service I can't select my own job? You can try this on some punk that's never been in the war effort, never done anything, but not on me!'

"And by this time, of course, I'm talking real loud. We're in one of those offices where there's a lot of low partition walls, and everybody is sticking his head up to see what is going on. But I got that job.

"All I really wanted was to get back to the Bush and out of that big mess I'd been in for three years. And I went right straight up to Yellowknife, in February 1943."

7

YELLOWKNIFE DAYS

The winter of 1943 was tough for flying. At first Boffa piloted the Norseman, BDF, and was more or less steadily on the Eldorado run to Great Bear Lake from Yellowknife. Freddy Miller was CPAir agent then; it was the beginning of a working relationship which lasted for many years.

From his very first run north to the uranium mine, which was producing vital wartime products, Ernie never once turned back to home base after setting out on the Eldorado run.

"I never returned on that trip, never aborted. I didn't get through, lots of times, but I stopped and camped out, never came back. By golly, the fellows before me had made 11 false starts! They'd get almost as far as Bear Lake, sometimes in sight of it, and then come all the way back home. Bad weather turned them back and they had to have a place to sleep. But I camped right out in the open. It was a real bad winter, with some terrible weather conditions, a lot of fog and icy crud around Bear Lake. We got the weather conditions from there by radio, but it could change again before you got there.

"Finally I talked Eldorado Mines and CPAir into putting a couple of camps in on the way from Yellowknife to the mine, because we carried passengers sometimes, and you sure don't want to make them camp out in the snow. So they agreed. Eldorado put up the building material and paid two men to do the work, and CPAir put up the time required to haul the stuff into the sites. Martin Bode and George Bryson, two good carpenters from Yellowknife, put up the camps for me, one on Matt Berry Lake and the other at Grant Lake, about one-third and two-thirds of the way.

"By golly, that was a cinch then; when the weather got bad you could either skim along and get into Grant or come back to Matt Berry Lake, but you didn't need to come all the way back to Yellowknife. We kept emergency grub there, cots and mattresses, stove, a real nice setup in those log cabins."

Before they got the cabins built, however, Ernie had enjoyed his first game of "brick" bridge. Flying back from Coppermine with a mechanic and his passenger, Father Gathy, the weather turned sour so they sat down at Grant Lake. Ernie set up a tent. There was a load of firebrick sitting there waiting to be taken into Eldorado, so he used it to build a table for the primus stove. After supper, he built another table and they played three-handed bridge, with the good father excelling as usual. He had been a professional magician in Belgium before joining the Oblate fathers.

"We talked about that for a long time," Ernie grins. "I'd run into him on the street in Yellowknife and Father Gathy would say, 'How about some brick bridge, Ernie?' He was a great guy. There are a lot of great stories about him — make a whole book, I guess. It was said he'd been in the Intelligence Corps of the Belgian army during the first war and had been captured as a spy by the Germans. He was lined up against a wall to be shot, blindfolded and the whole bit, and I guess it was a pretty desperate situation. He started saying his prayers and promised the Almighty if He could find a way out of the mess, he'd devote the rest of his life to the church. For some reason, the firing squad didn't shoot, and sure enough, he joined the Oblate Order later.

"We heard that now and then, when the Oblates needed money, Gathy would get special permission to go on a tour as a magician again, packing the halls and raising real dough. Anyway, after he came out to Canada, he was a great priest for the North, not too strict with the backsliders and always kind. For instance, when Gerry Murphy died, a Protestant and a Mason to boot, Father Gathy got special permission from his bishop and conducted the final services for his friend."

There were a lot of colorful characters around the gold mining camps in those days. Veterans hurried North as soon as they got out of uniform because there was a real gold boom on in Yellowknife in 1945. Many joyful reunions took place on the paths around the Rock in the old town, wartime separation over and old friends shouting one another's names. Every such reunion, of course, had to be celebrated in the nearest watering hole, despite the rationed beer and the requirement to bring your own log to sit on in the old town beer parlor.

When E.J.B. first went up to Yellowknife, he was on his own for a few months, with Nettie and the children still down south in Prince Albert, so after flying hours he spent quite a lot of time in Vic Ingraham's hotel. Three other cronies in those days were Jock McMeekan, who was prospecting, promoting and publishing his mimeographed sheet, the *Yellowknife Blade;* his staking partner named McKinnon; and Ward Treadway, with whom Boffa was setting up the Tartan Syndicate to promote the sale of gold claims.

There was sometimes a clerk from the Bank of Commerce (much like Robert W. Service, Ernie recalls) and barber Les Gray, who liked to read poetry. These creative (and unlikely) men composed stuff which later became known throughout the North.

It was Les Gray who originated the song, the chorus of which ran, "Oh you can't go to heaven, on CPA/Cause they just fly the other way," for which anyone could compose his own appropriate verses, and some nights they went on and on and on. One might start, "Vic Ingraham runs the Yellowknife bar/Got lots of beer, but no Old Paar," and the next customer would carry on with, "The beer is bad and the service is worse/And Sleepy Jim sleeps while we're dyin' of thirst." The next chorus might be, "You can't go to heaven when you leave the Snye/You go down north and there you die," and it would wind up with "Oh, you can't go to heaven on the MRT[Mackenzie River Transportation Company]/ Unless you work for the HBC." Life had its lighter moments.

Ernie swears there was one occasion when somebody fresh in from the Bush dragged Les Gray out of bed to come down to the bar and give him a haircut. Les came protesting, in his pajamas, and didn't get out of the place for the next three days and nights!

When Vic Ingraham, prospering with the boom, built his big new establishment up in the new government-planned town site, Rose and Del Curry, two northern pioneers, ran the old hotel down on the Rock. No one but Rose can do full justice to the story of coming down the steep back steps of the hotel with a honeybucket brimming full, when she tripped. But for years afterward, all you had to ask was, "Did you ever get hit with a bucket?" and the real old-timers would break into whoops of laughter.

Flying for CPAir out of Yellowknife during the staking boom was right down Ernie's alley. He had an uncanny knack for finding his way to the secret gold rush sites, where claim stakers headed by charter flight. Often, they would not divulge their destination until the plane was in the air, suspicious even of the dispatcher in the air-radio hut. No one must get there ahead of them! This practice led more than once to serious consequences, when a pilot would drop a prospector or two off at some secret lakeshore, promising to come back and pick them up at a specified time. In at least one case, because the original pilot was away on holiday, no one in the charter office knew where to go to find them. Fred Giauque and his sons, for example, nearly starved to death out in the Bush, until one of them walked back to Yellowknife through the muskeg and took out a rescue plane. After that, Giauque bought his own plane!

John Parker, a young lawyer establishing a practice in Yellowknife then, was involved in some of the mining ventures. Years later, retired from the bench and living in Vancouver, he recalled Boffa's uncanny ability to locate himself on that water-pocked landscape out of Yellowknife. On one occasion Parker and another northerner chartered the Norseman for a staking trip without revealing their destination. After they took off from Yellowknife Bay and were away from the town, they handed Boffa a map, folded down to a six-inch square, and pointed to one of a hundred small lakes on that section.

"There," they said. "That's where we want to go."

Ernie took the map in one hand, flying with the other, looked at it closely, and shook his head. "Can't figure out where that is," he said doubtfully. Then his face lit up, he turned the map upside down to its correction position, and said, "Oh, you mean there!" And off they went.

Looking back now, Ernie says he wasn't any wizard.

"It was easy, because all the staking went on not too far from Yellowknife," he says. "It was mostly within a radius of 20 or 30 miles. You didn't have to be a wizard after flying around there for a year or so, taking prospectors all over the place. Surely you'd recognize those lakes."

But it wasn't just around Yellowknife. Passengers who flew confidently with Ernie were comforted by the knowledge that he knew every trapper's cabin and every campsite along the route as they

Yellowknife, on Great Slave Lake, was growing up "the Rock" in the 1940s as the hub of a gold boom in Northwest Territories.
(Jim Whyard)

headed out into those cold, wintry wastes, whether their destination was Eldorado or Coppermine or elsewhere.

And in the summer it was just as comforting to know that your pilot wouldn't get lost among the myriads of lakes and streams; if you ran into bad weather, he'd fix up a comfortable tent camp as fast as you could say muskeg. Because of the long northern summer days, flying continued around the clock, and the noise of bush craft roaring off the water or taxiing into the narrows to tie up at the dock never seemed to cease. Sometimes a new engine would be put in right there at the dock, and then be run in for hours and hours, until eardrums became immune to the roar. Ernie says it couldn't have been any worse for the eardrums than rock-'n'-roll records or snowmobiles are today.

That first summer of 1943, E.J.B. was flying prospectors and staking parties in and out to the Bush for American Metals, and the following year he looked after four prospecting parties for the same company. Then in 1945 he was flying young geologists up to the Coppermine Hills and into the company's camp at Dismal Lakes. As always, he soaked up every bit of knowledge like a sponge, and became familiar with geological terms and prospecting information. It all came in handy later, when he went prospecting on his own and with Jake Woolgar.

It wasn't just prospectors and mining people who were using

CPAir in those days, however, and Ernie tells some fascinating stories about flying trappers back to the Bush each year.

"In late August all these Barren Lands trappers go back to the Barrens and spend the winter trapping. You got to get them there early enough so they can put up their firewood, scrub spruce, stuff like that. Most of them had camps close to where there was some spruce they could cut and stack up, just like stacking hay. It takes a lot of that fuel to see you through the winter, so they went in early.

"We'd leave from Fort Reliance for the Slave Lake bunch, but we also flew some in from Camsell Portage, near Goldfields on Lake Athabasca [in northern Saskatchewan], and from Stoney Rapids, where another bunch would leave from the Saskatchewan end of it.

"There would be maybe 10 or more trappers, with all their dogs, all their gear, everything they'd need for the winter. You can imagine the barking and howling that went on. The dogs were all staked out in their camps; each family had its own tent in this spot, back on a point across the bay from the police barracks at Fort Reliance. So CPAir would have a bunch of gas stored there, barrels and a wobble pump [portable hand pump].

"Away we'd go. Fill her up with gas and load all these dogs into the plane. First of all, we'd put in all the gear — flour, groceries and stuff — then the guy would get in with the dogs and he'd sit there with a club in his hand, ready to clobber them if they started fighting or anything.

"That brings to mind a story. I think it was Gilmore; he was out there flying trappers one time and he had a Fairchild 71. He got this great load in — we were always overloaded, you know. These fellows couldn't make two trips — they couldn't afford two trips — so you'd just simply load everything and go. Well, this 71 couldn't quite handle it all. It was really low in the water and, to top it all off, the load slid back.

"So the aircraft tail was going into the water, sinking backward, and he had to open her up full to keep her from doing that — it was only the blast from the propeller on the tail end that kept his tail up. He couldn't slow down until he got on the other side of the lake, to shallow water where he could shut her off and reorganize the load!

"Well, we just kept gassing up and flying a load at a time out to the trapping camps. Most of the time you just got one trip in during the day. If the guys were closer in you could sometimes make two trips in a day, but, oh, that is about the nicest time of year in the Barren Lands, in the fall. Just getting to the stage where the moss and willow leaves start to turn, and the caribou are just losing the velvet, their antlers are partly bloody where the velvet is being scraped off. You land on this lake, and you can be taxiing toward shore and you see nothing but willows. All of a sudden there's an outline of a caribou. You talk about camouflage, boy, it's perfect, and when you see one you look around and you might see a whole herd there, but they don't show up unless they're against the skyline. But it's beautiful, that time of year, red, yellow, orange . . .

"This one time we had a very strong wind. We pulled up to unload this trapper and his gear in the narrow bay. I kept the engine running, just nosed up to shore, which wasn't good enough to move up on, too rocky. I had to hold her there while they tied up. I had Tommy Clark with me and he didn't usually move too fast. So I said, 'How about it, all set?' He said, 'Yes, all set,' and I turned off. And, by golly, she broke loose — they hadn't tied her very well — and started drifting backward, and right then my starter switch went haywire. She wouldn't start.

"Here I am, going tail first, blown by the wind toward this rocky shore and the wind was really blowing! And here's Tommy, just running for all he's worth — he had a pair of those sheeplined overshoes on, not fastened up, flopping away at each step, running around that bay. I don't think he ever moved that fast in his life before. And I'm out on the tail end of the float with a paddle, ready to try to slow her down.

"He got there and walked right into the water and I jumped off the float and together we stopped her from going on the rocks. So then we had to take the switch out to fix it and keep the plane from pounding on the rocks. I remember we got some bolts off an old sled runner we found near the camp. We rigged a switch, put it on, and, by golly, it worked. We started her up, taxied over to the camp, and unloaded the trapper's gear."

On his many flights to the coast, to points such as Coppermine, Ernie got to know many of the native hunters and trappers, and became a sort of agent for some of them, years before any government agency was interested in helping them develop their own fur trading business.

"Occasionally I would go into a place and a guy would have a polar bear. Hudson's Bay Company would buy it from him right there, but they didn't pay too much, so I used to bring it out and get the best price I could for him. I got so I was handling quite a few polar bears. At that time, Jimmy Kear, who used to fly for CPAir, was in Edmonton. I'd ship them to him and he'd sell them out there.

"So I kept looking for a good one for myself, and finally I got one, the nicest one I have ever seen, silvery white and beautiful.

*Journalists from everywhere came to the Boffas' door in Yellowknife.
Here Australian Mrs. Frank Clune sits for her writer-husband with
Ernie, son Joe, Nettie (right front), and Flo Whyard.* (Frank Clune)

And I told Jimmy, 'Now that one is for me, just get it tanned and
made up, don't you dare sell it!'

"And, by golly, he sold it. I never did get one for myself."

E.J.B. was also instrumental in bringing out the earliest pieces
of Eskimo soapstone carvings, before the Canadian government
got around to sending in James Houston to instruct and encourage
the carvers. A teacher at Coppermine urged some of the local people
to try carving the stone they found nearby, and Ernie brought out
some of their work to Yellowknife. Here their artistry was recognized by Didi Woolgar, an early northern handicraft supporter,
one of the founders of the local branch of the Canadian Handicraft
Guild and owner of one of the first Yellowknife shops. She found
a ready market for the work, some of which became museum pieces.

These were aboriginal art pieces, Eskimos doing their own thing, with no one teaching them how. Now, of course, it has grown into an important industry across the Arctic, and the carvings are world famous.

Another new interest for Boffa was reading the narratives of the early explorers in the Mackenzie and coastal areas of the country over which he was now flying. He became fascinated by their first-hand tales of hardship and desperate courage. One of his objectives for years was to visit some of the sites of camps made by survivors of the Franklin expeditions. He read everything he could get his hands on, and now owns one of the finest private collections of such history.

That explains the Signal Corps message delivered to Captain E. Boffa, CPAir, Yellowknife, late one August by the government of Canada's Radiotelegraph Service. The message read, "Have moved camp Back River to Dismal Lakes stop Expect you about end of this century stop Kindly reserve 70 rooms Ingraham's new hotel for my party and 1 for Sam Hearne stop Make railroad reservations Yellowknife to Edmonton. Franklin."

It was from Phil Jenney of American Metals, and reading between the lines, E.J.B. says, "It was his way of telling me to get off my butt and get up there! I was doing all his flying at that time, up in Coppermine Hills, and I camped there, traveled around contacting prospectors. Phil was interested in the Arctic and its explorers too; we used to talk about those exploration parties all the time. I was beginning to get this collection of books and I'd pick up one of these books and we'd read about these people, Franklin and Hearne and so on. So this signal was just his way of telling me to get cracking."

It's hard to understand why anyone would need to tell Boffa to get cracking. If you talk to men who were his mechanics or young crew members back in the Yellowknife days, it doesn't sound as if he ever took a minute off the job.

John Dennison remembers heading for Gordon Lake on a search trip with Sandy Tweed. Karl Holm had been out on the trap line four or five days, with no food, sleeping bag nor camping gear, searching for his partner. The weather closed in and Dennison and Tweed flew back to Yellowknife. Ernie met them with this message, "You don't come back. You land and you wait out the weather when a man's life is at stake."

So they loaded the stinking dogs and headed for Salmita Mine. On December 20, they made an overnight camp, and in the early morning darkness, Boffa's mechanic started up the blow pots right underneath the plane.

71

"Ernie zoomed out of that tent and down to that airplane practically in his bare feet," Dennison says with a grin. "I never saw anyone move so fast! And that poor kid sure wished he was someplace else while he was being chewed out. But he learned and he sure never made that mistake again!"

Christmas of 1946 Dennison recalls spending at the Salmita campsite, six of them in one tent. Their search had located only tracks made by Holm's missing partner, 20 miles out on the lake, heading due south. The trap line ran between Courageous Lake and Aylmer Lake. They gave up the search. The missing trapper was never found, and had no relatives to pursue the mystery.

As for Sandy Tweed, the little boy who had soloed at Lethbridge at the age of 11, son of Boffa's good friend — he had to wait a few years to get his license. He started flying for CPAir in 1943 at Peace River, on a Travelair 6000 on the mail run, then spent a winter in Quebec and landed in Yellowknife in the spring of 1946. He flew out of there on and off for the next three years, then went to Norman Wells, the last bush operation the company had. Tweed flew out of Edmonton, then went international and was a senior pilot on CPAir overseas jet flights when he retired from 747s, a far cry from the northern days with Boffa.

Sandy Tweed had lived and breathed airplanes, like his father before him. As a boy at Lethbridge airport, he recalled, they opened the kitchen door right into the hangar, and if you went out the front door there were airplanes parked on the grass.

Circuit court officials from Prince Albert wait out a forced landing as Boffa finds the culprit — a scrap of paper in the Fox Moth's gas tank!

Twin buildings on Yellowknife Narrows housed a government liquor store and mining recorder's office, with staff living quarters above.

In an interview at Whitehorse in the fall of 1980, Captain Tweed (then senior pilot and partner in his son Bill's company, Simpson Air, based at Fort Nelson, British Columbia) willingly talked about E.J. Boffa. He said, "As far as I'm concerned, Ernie is the finest pilot that ever flew an airplane. I'm not talking today's precision flying, but he knew the limits of the machine he was flying right down to one mile an hour. No one else could do it so effectively. He could take it past that limit if he had to, he knew it so well. Not just that particular aircraft, but any airplane he flew. He could get more out of that damn airplane than anybody else could. He's a natural pilot."

Speaking of the changes since the early bush pilot days, Tweed said, "I don't know that there's a great deal of difference, but as far as the average pilot is concerned, he hasn't got the capability of taking care of the airplane in the same way Ernie Boffa did. If Ernie happened to bend something, or break something, he could stop and fix it and then keep on going. The average pilot today doesn't have the mechanical ability to do that. Even if he had the mechanical ability he wouldn't have the knowledge of how far he could go with this thing and still complete the operation."

One of his favorite stories about E.J.B.'s flying in the north concerned the Bellanca, when Sandy was flying as Ernie's young helper. Sandy remembered, "The big Bellanca's direction control, landing on a smooth, icy surface, left something to be desired. In soft snow, fine, but on the Canol strip, where the darn thing was effectively glare ice, it was a little difficult keeping the airplane on the strip.

"So what I would do — I always rode in the right front seat of this thing — I'd go out the door and down the leading edge of the lift strut and back to the trailing edge. The lift strut on the

73

Bellanca was very wide . . . and from there I would jump and catch the lift strut on the tail and swing up underneath it and get my feet onto the tail ski, normally one foot on the nose of the ski and the other on the tail of the ski, and by watching the air rudder I could see where he wanted the airplane to go and I could steer the airplane that way! I got fairly adept at this; you know, I can only remember falling off the darn thing once. Away went the airplane, and of course, Ernie gave me hell because I fell off!

"You had to get on the tail when it was moving fairly quickly, coming in on a landing, I would guess 30 or 40 miles per hour, but no slipstream from the prop. It would be a full idle and quite often he'd have to give the prop a blast, kick it a little bit, but there'd be very little from the prop. But the big thing, of course, was the flying snow, coming off the skis, and trying to keep your parka hood out of your eyes so you could see.

"You did the break, caught the strut and swung around, hanging with both arms, got your feet on the ski, and held your parka out of your eyes with your fingertips. I got pretty adept at it after a while. I don't know if anyone else perfected that system, but Ernie and I had it down to a science. We were a pretty good team.

"I'd go out the door when he gave me the signal. I'd get the message, be out the door, down the wing and onto the tail, all in a matter of seconds, if I caught it right. If I missed it, of course, I was of no use to him and just got left behind at the airport.

"They weren't just Boffa's orders, you know," Tweed said seriously. "We worked it out together. We knew we needed something to help steer that tail. If we went off the runway into the snow we were in deep trouble. We would have to go and get equipment to come and pull us out. I don't recall that we ever went off that runway. Our split-second timing worked out quite well!" And the veteran of international jet flights beamed proudly as he recalled that early success with Boffa.

"Yes," he repeated quietly. "In my opinion, Ernie Boffa was the finest pilot that ever flew an airplane."

At Yellowknife, E.J.B. was certainly the right man in the right spot at the right time.

— 8 —
SEARCH AND RESCUE

The one thing that could chill the heart of every northerner in those early days was the news that a plane was missing — particularly in the winter months.

Most of the pilots and their families were known personally in Yellowknife; they were friends and neighbors. Their safety was a matter of concern to hundreds of people. Once a search began there was no other topic of conversation until it had ended.

Ernie Boffa knew about searching for lost aircraft — from both sides of the story. Sometimes it was all over before word got out, but, once in a while, the story became a headliner, and for a few days the eyes of all Canadians turned northward. One such search occurred at Christmas in 1945.

Ernie had gone to Montreal that December to pick up a new Norseman for CPAir. In his absence, pilot Jack Herriot and mechanic Gordie Brown were flying the regular trip to Coppermine, taking mail, freight and Inspector L.A. Learmonth of the Hudson's Bay Company. The Norseman CF-CPS reached Eldorado safely from Yellowknife December 18, and left at 1:25 P.M. for Coppermine, where everyone was in high spirits awaiting Christmas mail. The temperature was 30° below zero, and there was very little daylight. At 3:25 P.M. the plane had not arrived, though the usual flight time was about an hour and a half. Then the radio operator at Coppermine heard CPS reporting to Eldorado that they could not find Coppermine and were circling.

The men in the arctic settlement quickly made flares, lit up the ice runway, put flare pots along the strip, and set up flares on the hill behind the settlement. But at four o'clock the pilot, who still hadn't spotted the buildings through the ground mist, decided to land on a small lake 30 or 40 miles south of Coppermine. The plane did not arrive the following day, and on the 20th, Coppermine alerted CPAir officials in Yellowknife.

Meanwhile Boffa was flying happily home from Montreal with his new plane, and Nettie and the three kids, Kay, Joan, and little Joe, born in Yellowknife in 1945, were expecting him for Christmas. As soon as he hit the runway at Yellowknife he heard the news about Herriot and Learmonth, a friend of Boffa's from his many trips north for Hudson's Bay. The next morning, December 22, Coppermine got the word that Captain Boffa was on the way in the new Norseman, BHV, picking up Dr. Baker at Eldorado, who had volunteered to help in the search.

To quote William McLean's story of the search in the *Beaver*, the Hudson's Bay Company magazine:

> *Everyone was greatly relieved at this news, as Captain Boffa's reputation was known by all as a careful and skillful pilot, who immediately imbues his passengers with confidence and a sense of security. En route to Coppermine, from Eldorado, Captain Boffa carefully scrutinized the Coppermine River and its environs, turning off at Bloody Falls to closely watch the lakes and Nipartoktuak River to its mouth. Landing at Coppermine just before darkness, he reported he had found no traces of the missing flight.*
>
> *After a general conference, it was decided that he would search an area 25 to 30 miles wide on either side of the Coppermine River, south to the Coppermine and September Mountains. By 10:00 P.M. it was apparent that the thin stratus cloud formation would disperse, allowing a full moon to light up the terrain sufficiently for takeoff. But shortly afterward, further stratus rolled in from the west and south, and it was decided everyone would turn in. The radio operator who had the 4:00 A.M. weather sched would awaken Boffa and his mechanic, Mike Zupko.*

At four in the morning of December 23, the weather had cleared to perfect visibility and the moon was brilliant. Boffa and Zupko quickly warmed up the BHV, flares were lit on the runway on the sea ice and on the hilltop, and they took off at 20 minutes past 4. They flew four hours but spotted no fires anywhere, except their own signal flare on the hill, so returned to refuel, then took off again at ten and covered an even wider area, still with no results. Ernie decided more help was needed, and he called Yellowknife.

Down in Edmonton, Alf Caywood had also been preparing to enjoy Christmas with his family, but he took off to help in the search, as did Wop May.

Caywood, the pilot for Eldorado Mining Company, had himself been forced down in the Barrens for nine days in the winter of 1941, when his aircraft caught fire in midair and his passenger, Paddy

Gibson, was killed. He arrived in Yellowknife at half past three December 24 and took off again immediately with Wop May, a veteran bush pilot who was then superintendent of CPAir at Edmonton, then arrived at Eldorado just before dark. Pilot Roy McHaffie in BDF also set out for Coppermine via Eldorado, with additional search equipment.

Meanwhile Boffa had continued his aerial search out of Coppermine, and thought he heard weak CW signals calling BHV just when his gas was running low. Returning to the strip, he refueled, picked up McLean, and went back to where he heard the signal, but nothing was detected. Dejectedly he turned his plane back to Coppermine; he was tired and discouraged.

After a good night's sleep, Boffa awoke on Christmas Day determined to proceed farther into unmapped country south and east of Coppermine, taking Dr. Baker along with him about ten. In the meantime, Alf Caywood with Wop May in BTW and Roy McHaffie and Len De Blocq had left Eldorado and were searching the area from the Kendall River northward and east of Coppermine, contacting Boffa by radio to make sure each knew the other's whereabouts and plans.

Proceeding farther south and east, Boffa circled over each lake and searched every angle from a height of four hundred feet. After he had reached the large lake inland that he had mapped out as the farthest point of his search, he turned westward and slightly south — and, suddenly, at a quarter past eleven was flying right over the barely visible missing aircraft! Only the outline of the plane, covered by frost and snow, could be guessed at as Boffa taxied up to the plane. Two figures finally emerged from the downed aircraft, waving, safe and well, after eight long and bitterly cold days and nights. It was Christmas Day, 1945.

They had the blow pot going in the plane's cabin and hadn't heard the aircraft overhead.

To quote William McLean again:

> *Boffa set his ship down on the small lake about half a mile from CPS and grinned his delight as he relaxed in his seat after four days and nights of constant vigil. He had flown some 30 hours on the search, a good 12 hours by moonlight, so great was his feeling of urgency. Pilot Herriot stood beaming with delight, throwing apish kisses at Boffa in appreciation of their rescue. As soon as the motor had been shut off, Dr. Baker accompanied Herriot back to CPS, where Learmonth had suffered a frozen foot during the ordeal.*

CPS had run into jagged rocks sticking up through the snow when their emergency landing had been made in the near dark, and the coating of brass had been rubbed off the skis onto these rocks, leading to one moment of excitement when the downed men thought they had discovered gold! Without a tent, fur clothing, nor even a snow knife to make a shelter, they had to survive within the aircraft, which was poor protection against the December cold.

Half an hour after landing, Boffa took off with the three extra passengers on board BHV, circled, and plotted the location of CPS for repair crews who would later repair the broken starter shaft and charge the battery, then flew back to Coppermine, where the entire population waited to greet them.

Before heading back to Edmonton that afternoon, Caywood presented two roasted turkeys to Mrs. McLean and Mrs. Webster, the only white women in the settlement, a gift from manager Bolger of Eldorado Mines. The ladies soon had things organized in the kitchen and when everything was ready, 18 people sat down at a long table in the RCMP detachment, and joined with Canon H.J. Webster in his prayer of thanksgiving for a successful outcome to the search. At the conclusion of the dinner, a toast was proposed by Inspector Learmonth to Captain Boffa and the CPAir men who had left their homes and families to find their friends.

Later, at home in Yellowknife, Ernie received a silver cigarette case from the Hudson's Bay Company, in appreciation of his efforts that December of 1945. Ernie just says, "Hell, they would have done the same for me," which leads to another story.

Late in May of 1949, after piloting the first tuberculosis survey across the Arctic, Ernie rented an Anson to fly Mr. and Mrs. Linc Washburn of the Arctic Institute of America on a special charter to Holman Island. They left Yellowknife with a full load, carrying not only the Washburns and their gear for a summer's work, plus mechanic Fred Riley, but also HBC shipments destined for Reid Island and Coppermine as well as Holman.

At Eldorado Ernie changed to skis for the Anson because winter conditions still applied north from there.

"We went through some weather after that," Ernie recalls. "Nothing too bad, but not very good, and broke out of it north of Reid Island. We couldn't land there, and went direct to Holman, where we off-loaded the Washburns and their gear. We gassed up at Holman; Fred Riley filled both tanks, because we needed enough to get back to Eldorado.

"So away we go, south again, and we ran into weather there in the Dolphin Strait at the south end of Victoria Island. I was pretty tired, and we were into this low fog that just sits and doesn't move. But we could get up over it, and kept going. Then one tank ran out, so I switched over — and the gauge showed just a little bit of gas!

"I said, 'I thought you filled these tanks?' And Fred said, 'I filled them both,' and it was sure funny, because the gauge showed nearly empty. And another thing — the battery regulator didn't work, the wires were crossed somewhere; it was boiling and we could smell acid in the aircraft. So, what were we going to do?

"We're more than halfway from Holman to Eldorado by now, on a track roughly west of Coppermine, in a hell of a lot of low fog. I know we're flying over a fairly flat plateau, and soon we'll be getting into the hills. So I decided to let her down gradually through the fog and take a look at a landing place.

"Well, I wasn't really familiar with that Anson, and I let down just a bit too fast; but I was watching very carefully, and although you couldn't really see through that fog, it looked like a white space underneath, like a big, frozen lake, so I let her down some more, and we hit — crack! We busted the undercarriage. We hit at a shallow angle, not nosed in, just the skis, and I gunned it, figuring I was on the ground with what looked like ice all around me — then I chopped it and set her down, and, of course, all hell broke loose when we hit the drifts. The engines were the lowest things on the plane and they caught, you know, and out went the engines before we stopped.

"The thing turned around and was heading the other way — ground-looped a little bit — but there wasn't a mark on the wings or cabin or anywhere. We lived in it for three days, had lots of food and a primus stove. We were actually living like kings. We had eggs, meat and fruit on board — a whole lot of bananas, too, that were headed for Reid and Coppermine but couldn't get in there to unload, and were bringing it back to take in on the next trip.

"But the fog wouldn't let up, and we just sat there for two days. The radio didn't work, and it was hard to see just where we were. Finally, on the third day, it cleared enough so we could start walking. We made toboggans out of the cowling, loaded grub and sleeping bags, tied some cable to pull them, and headed southeast. Along the way we put up cairns of rocks and snow, to guide us back if the fog moved in again.

"As soon as we got to some high ground, I recognized the ridges — they extend west from Coppermine, a series of basalts, with a peculiar taper — and I knew right away we were north of Rae River, not very far west of Coppermine. So we headed southeast and started to walk to Coppermine.

"Got about seven or eight miles and we heard the first plane east of us, going north, so I said to Riley, 'We'd better go back, they can't help but spot our airplane. So we walked back and we weren't there long before the RCAF was overhead.

"Our radio needed a tube, so I wrote the serial number in the snow, and, by golly, they dropped exactly the right one into the snow, wrapped up well in a sleeping bag. So we fixed up the radio and then we could talk to them. We told them not to land without skis, and they said that was O.K., there was a DC-3 coming equipped with skis. And they circled overhead and wouldn't go away and leave us until another aircraft arrived. I told them, if they didn't want to land, it was O.K., we could walk to Coppermine, but they said no way, and dropped a couple of bales of stuff for us, everything you could imagine."

They were all back at Sawmill Bay, Eldorado, at midnight. Flight-Lieutenant Peter Gibb, who had circled overhead for three hours, had returned to Sawmill after one of the four-engine Lancasters helping in the search took over at the crash site. Then Gibb flew back in a ski-wheel-equipped Dakota which had been flown in from Rivers, Manitoba, and completed the rescue operation, dropping down to pick up Boffa and Riley and return them to the search base at Sawmill Bay.

E.J.B. expressed his sincere thanks, and that of Fred Riley, in a letter to Air Vice Marshal Hugh Campbell, Air Officer Commanding, Northwest Air Command, a few days later. Part of his letter said:

> As a direct result of your efficient organization, our rescue was carried out in record time and under extreme weather conditions in a snow-covered area which made landing and takeoff extremely precarious . . .
>
> To Squadron Leader Miller, who coordinated the search, Flight-Lieutenant Gibb who captained the rescuing aircraft, to the ground crew at Fort Nelson responsible for maintaining the search craft, the crew of the ski-wheel-equipped Dakota which was rushed from Rivers, Manitoba, to land on the isolated spot, and to the men on the Lancaster which covered such an area during the search, I would especially like to convey our gratitude.

Ernie doesn't say so, but the fact that he had left complete details of his flight plan with the Washburns, and his alternative routes in case of bad weather, made the task a whole lot simpler.

Washburn got in touch with the RCAF when he heard that the Anson was missing, and their search area could then be put within specific boundaries. That surely helped.

There's a certain pattern followed by most pilots who are downed in wilderness areas and know they'll have to depend on others to be found. At least, it applied years ago before modern electronic communication devices did much to simplify the searchmaster's work.

Ernie tells about searching for pilot Jack Moar during the 1940s at Yellowknife. "One of his young pilots had gone to Wrigley and broken a ski or some such thing and Jack Moar was on his way with the Anson to Wrigley to fix him up. He ran into weather on the east side of those hills, east of the Mackenzie, south of Wrigley, and he couldn't get over those hills. The weather socked in badly so he sat down on a lake there.

"Moar and his crewman started to walk to shore, to pick out a place to camp overnight, when they turned around and saw, to their horror, that the aircraft was starting to sink down through the ice! They ran back, got all the stuff they could out of the plane — which was too far down by then to be moved — and it sank to its wings in the water.

"I went up looking for them. It was still socked in, and I got as close as I could to those lakes but couldn't get in, so had to go on to Wrigley. I picked up the young pilot there and the next morning it cleared enough and I went right straight to this lake and there he was.

"We dropped him a note, told him to mark a place where I could come in, something solid, near the shore, so he did that. In the meantime, I didn't want to go in there with too much weight, so I landed on another lake, good and solid, and unloaded everything I could. Then we went over and picked up Jack and his passenger.

"Funny thing about it, now they'd been there about three days or so and he had quite a nice little setup, quite a comfortable camp. I had a bottle of rum with me so we stopped and had a hot rum. I said, 'Gee, you've got a nice little camp here,' and Jack said, 'Yeah, it's kind of surprising. The first day after it happened, everything is a mess. You feel terrible, you know you've pulled a boner, leaving that plane on the ice like that. When we came to shore, any old thing would do, that first night. Then the next day, you've got lots of time to think it over, and you get more interested in fixing a nice camp. And then you get pretty fussy by the third day and keep on improving things.' "

One search, which was more frustrating and annoying than most of the others in which he was involved, reinforced Ernie's theory that you're always better on your own without having to rely upon any other aircraft or pilot. It was in the summer of 1948 when Boffa was on one of his annual charters with Margaret Oldenburg (more later about her). They wanted to get in and have a look around Back River at some of the camps made by Franklin's men, as well as gather botanical species there for Miss Oldenburg's university collection.

At Bathurst Inlet, where they had stopped to refuel after flying up from Yellowknife, they met two young Americans, Bud and Connie Helmericks, flying a little Cessna 140 (called *Arctic Tern*) with an 85 horsepower Continental engine, which could cruise at about 22 miles to the gallon. Over supper at the Hudson's Bay Company post that evening, Boffa suggested that they team up, make a base camp in the region they wanted to explore, then let the Cessna fly Miss Oldenburg out on short field trips and save gas for the heavier Norseman. This fitted in with the Helmerickses' plans; they were exploring on their own, filming the North for a lecture tour they were to make the following year.

The two planes took off in the late summer evening light, the Norseman leading the way on the course the two pilots had plotted on the kitchen table with their maps. Because they were faster, Ernie, Miss Oldenburg, and mechanic Dick Hahn sat down on a bay of MacAlpine Lake and waited for the smaller craft to catch

The Bellanca AWR lands on Great Slave Lake, where mail and freight are transferred to dog sleds. Teams are kept apart to avoid dog fights. (Courtesy CPAir)

up, then led the way into an already scouted landing on the large body of water known as Lakes Pelly and Garry. They tied up in a rocky cove overnight, and set up a tent camp.

After breakfast the next morning, Bud Helmericks took Margaret Oldenburg off in his *Arctic Tern* for a short flora-collecting jaunt around the immediate area, expecting to be back for lunch. They did not take warm clothing, sleeping bags nor gear, because it was to be a short flight only. They did not return.

Boffa waited impatiently all day, tramping around the rocky peninsula on which they were camped, shot a ptarmigan for the lunch pot, then flew over to talk to some Eskimo people camped farther along the lake. Back again to their mooring, there was still no small plane, and late that night it had to be admitted they were lost. E.J.B. figured out the odds, and what a search would require, worked out the gas available, and the hours he could fly before returning to Bathurst Inlet for refueling, then took off at four at first daylight to make a preliminary search of the area.

The whole region was a series of scrambled, winding arms of water, through part of which ran the legendary Back River, with scores of waterfalls and rapids. It was foggy and when the allotted search time was up, they headed for Bathurst, into even thicker fog, until they had to sit down and wait for it to clear. They reached Bathurst at noon, gassed up, lashed extra drums of gas into the cabin of the plane, and asked the Bay man to alert all arctic radio stations to stand by for a possible emergency. Then Ernie decided to wait until he completed one more trip inland before notifying CPAir that the plane was missing, which would mean a full-scale

search, calling out the RCAF and other complications. He commandeered all the air force gas cached at Bathurst, declaring that, in his judgment, it was an emergency and he couldn't afford to wait for permission.

He had given Bathurst the location of his camp, as closely as he could figure it in the unmapped country: 65°50′ north latitude, 101 west longitude, east of Bathurst, five hundred miles northwest of Hudson's Bay. They had picked up an Eskimo boy, Steve, to help check with local hunters and fishing camps they might find in the area. Ernie also discovered that the Helmerickses had no rescue insurance — had never heard of it, in fact.

Back at their camp there was still no sign of the *Arctic Tern,* and Boffa heard nothing on his radio throughout their flying time in the area.

The logistics were depressing. The Cessna's range was about 125 miles, but working out every possible course, that meant 49,062 square miles of possible search area. They started by searching the safe harbors, then along the shorelines everywhere, then up on the bare, rocky ground, then began looking for pieces of a plane. There was nothing.

Boffa had promised himself he would send out the go-ahead signal to Yellowknife the next morning if the missing plane wasn't found. But he couldn't get through on the radio, and, after a frustrating day, flew back to Bathurst, arriving in darkness, to learn that none of the "Alert" messages had been sent out to other stations because the wind-charger was down! Boffa blew his top and personally fixed the wind-charger and sent out the message. Everyone was tired, hungry and frustrated that night, sitting around in the kitchen of the Bay post. The next morning Ernie sent the call to Yellowknife for a search.

At two o'clock in the afternoon of the fourth day, they left again for the camp, unloaded extra gas drums, and made a special trip to an Eskimo camp where smoke was belching out of a tent — the eighth such camp they had dropped in on during the search — only to find the people had made the smoke just to get the plane to come down and visit with them. Back to base camp they flew, cooked a supper no one ate, and made plans to search that night, looking for a signal fire. Then a canoe came along the lake, Eskimos coming to call again — except that when one of them stuck his head inside the tent, it was Bud Helmericks.

The *Arctic Tern* had run out of gas that very first day, when he had flown about 115 miles out from camp, northeast, expecting because he had a headwind going out, he would have a tail wind coming back. The wind changed, and he was bucking a headwind, so instead of following the river home, he tried a shortcut, missed camp, and landed when his gas was gone. The next day, after a cold night in the small metal plane, Helmericks and the uncomplaining, good scout of a middle-aged botanist were pleased to welcome two Eskimos who had spotted the plane landing near their camp and come over to give a hand. One of them took Helmericks hunting and they got a caribou with the .22 rifle on board the plane; meat which they roasted on rocks heated by burning moss.

Each day they saw the Norseman in the distance, heading out to search, getting farther and farther away from where the *Arctic Tern* was sitting, west of Boffa's camp, not east where he was searching. So Helmericks and the Eskimos started paddling the Cessna around the shoreline in the general direction of Boffa's camp. They paddled across a bay, which he thought would take them to Pelly Lake, and nearly lost the airplane that night in a storm which banged the *Tern* up against the rocks in the rolling waves and wind. The next day Helmericks was led to yet another new Eskimo camp by his friends. When they heard the Norseman north of them, they patched up a canoe and traveled as fast as they could down the Back River in the cold night, to Boffa's camp.

Ernie lost no time in flying over to where the Cessna was tied up, taking gas for Helmericks to refuel, and bringing back Margaret Oldenburg six days after she had set out for a morning's botanical collecting. Time was running out on her annual charter, so they took off soon afterward for a quick run to the unmapped course of the Back River, tracing it to the coast. Back again at the camp the following night, they were ready to start for Bathurst Inlet. Helmericks refused to go in the stormy weather, so they all sat up in the tent and talked all night. With dawn the next morning, Boffa was ready to go, despite the fog and headwind.

At Bathurst they sent the word that the lost were found, ending the mishmash of exaggeration and incorrect information being headlined in the south. The Helmerickses said good-by to Boffa and Miss Oldenburg and headed for Coppermine; the Norseman was due back in Yellowknife and mechanic Dick Hahn was overdue for his own wedding down in Edmonton. Connie Helmericks made good copy out of the misadventure in her book, *The Flight of the Arctic Tern,* but was visibly put out, Ernie says, that her husband had got himself lost south of the Arctic Circle. It would have been so much more exciting in the Arctic!

On her part, Mrs. Helmericks wrote that Ernie Boffa was to arctic Canada what Sig Wien was to Alaska; that whenever anyone spoke of flying in the North, he spoke of Ernie Boffa in the same breath; probably no other living man had covered more arctic miles by air for the purpose of local commerce and mail carrying. He was famed for many rescues during his 23 years of northern flying — and whether she admitted it or not, Connie Helmericks was lucky to be flying with Boffa on that particular trip.

Bud Helmericks had obtained his license only three months before they headed into the Canadian north, and had made only three takeoffs on floats before picking up the new plane at Westport, Connecticut. They had begun their married life in Alaska, and said their profession was "exploration." Helmericks had learned to fly on a government grant, as a veteran of World War II. They were amazed at what they considered the lack of services for their aircraft as they made their way across Canada, after being accustomed to facilities for small planes throughout Alaska.

One Helmericks quote which still has Ernie Boffa shaking his head came from the annoyed young American who said in disgust one day, "How can we explore this country when you haven't any decent maps?"

Margaret Oldenburg, as usual, sailed through the experience unperturbed and oblivious to physical discomforts. Long before her side trip in the *Arctic Tern,* she had become a legend in her own time throughout the Canadian Arctic. The next chapter belongs to her.

OUTINGS WITH OLDENBURG

M argaret Oldenburg was a maiden lady of uncertain age but definite ideas. She knew what she wanted and was willing to pay the cost. Instead of traveling sedately around the world on cruise ships with elderly friends, this spinster librarian from Grand Marais, Minnesota, headed north to the Arctic on her own from 1939 to 1954.

That first year found her traveling on board SS *Nascopie*, which called at isolated Hudson's Bay Company posts with annual supplies, all the way into Churchill. Then she rode the railroad south to Winnipeg and home. In 1940 she was on another Bay boat, going down the Mackenzie River to Aklavik. Two years later she flew to Coppermine, then traveled by schooner to Aklavik. In 1943 she was on board a freight barge going down the Mackenzie to Aklavik. This time she spent the winter in that small arctic settlement, enjoyed it all immensely, and even produced a cookbook specializ-

Botanist Oldenburg, with pilot Boffa, seen here on one of the Blenkey Islands, added much to the world's knowledge of arctic flora.
(Len De Blocq)

ing in such exotic items as caribou headcheese and other native delicacies. Here she learned about Herschel Island and also visited Cambridge Bay.

But it was in 1945 that the winning combination of Boffa, a chartered CPAir bush plane, mechanic and Margaret Oldenburg first comes together. Margaret was not only an amateur botanist competent enough to collect for the University of Minnesota and the national botanist in Ottawa, she was also an arctic history buff; so was Ernie Boffa. Strangely enough, her chartered itineraries took them to places they both wanted to see. It was an ideal arrangement.

On that first charter from August 9 through 12, 1945, Captain Boffa and Miss Oldenburg took the *Barkley Grow* to Coppermine, Bernard Harbour, Reid Island, Holman Island Post, Melville and Victoria islands, then back again to Yellowknife. And it is up there, on the east side of Prince of Wales Strait, on the northwest tip of Victoria Island, Loch Point on the hydrographic map sheet, that Boffa called a small lake Oldenburg Lake for the first white woman to land there. He built a rock cairn with a tin can containing that message and has tried to get it officially recognized by Canadian map makers in Ottawa.

As well as collecting and pressing plants growing in the Arctic, Margaret kept a detailed journal from which she prepared reports on each of her summer jaunts. Here is an excerpt from the 1945 report:

> *At Coppermine, 10/8/45: Took on full load of fuel and put two drums of gas in cabin of plane. Takeoff delayed until storm waves had subsided. Reid Island reported too rough for landing so we went to Bernard Harbour. Wind easterly. Landed near RCAF gas cache. Because of rocks, plane could not get to land; mechanic and pilot waded ashore to examine gas cache. No further report from Reid received.*
>
> *Reid Island: In spite of the not entirely diminished wind and waves, Captain Boffa made a good landing. Perhaps the grounded ice did a little breakwater service . . . stopped here only long enough to refuel. I went ashore, but did no collecting, being busy greeting old friends. There were more Eskimo tents than I had ever seen here before.*
>
> *Holman Island Post: Consulted Natkusiat, who was on Melville with Stefansson. He reported Melville visible from Victoria (it was) and that lakes on Melville were few and shallow; also Winter Harbour was open long before*

the rest of the island. Another Eskimo indicated a six-foot-wide streak of copper (greenish) to be not far from the post. We flew direct to Walker Bay, over or in sight of rocky hills. No sign of our gas cache, so we went right on. . . .

What we could see of Prince of Wales Strait was all ice, very few open leads between Victoria and Melville — most of the ice was dark and snow flecked. Only when we were within 20 minutes or so of Winter Harbour did we see open water; the harbour, a few miles outside the harbour and to the south, was entirely open. We landed, with the sun shining, just below Captain Bernier's cache building, where there was a small boat. The mechanic waded ashore to bring it out but it leaked badly. We managed to ferry ashore the tent and food.

Despite the sun it was cold. Two or three hours later, when I started to collect, there was frost on the ground, but it did not affect the flowers which were blooming profusely. Musk ox tracks were very common — but we only saw three musk ox, all adults, grazing singly. A small gray fox (I thought it a cat at first) ran by us at the cache.

A pair of white wolves, with their tawny cubs, investigated me very thoroughly. They came first to where I had left my caribou parka and carton of specimens. The female nosed, but did not upset, the carton; picked up the parka and shook it a couple of times. She took some hair off it but did not tear it. When they came after me, they separated to come in at right angles and came up rather slowly; the male especially trying to keep under cover. At first he was the more aggressive, but after a couple of stones came at him, which he trotted over to and sniffed, he quit. The female came to about 12 feet from me, when a stone made her dodge. She stood sniffing a bit; then started slowly away with many pauses, looking back. They seemed in good condition.

Miss Oldenburg also noted rabbit and bear droppings, caribou prints, several long-tailed jaegers flying overhead, snowbirds and a sandpiper on the beach, and the print of a crane. There were a lot of lemming holes but no droppings, so apparently the holes were old ones. Bernier's cache building was in good condition but the contents were few and entirely spoiled. The cache door was off its hinges, braced shut by a heavy wheel and set of wagon springs. The incriptions on Monument Rock were still entirely legible.

Banks Island was discovered by Robert McClure in 1850, when he was searching for Sir John Franklin from the west. He sledged on over the ice to Viscount Melville Sound, completing the discovery of the Northwest Passage. The 1945 flight to the north end of Banks Island was the farthest north Boffa ever had flown; the magnet was Parry's Winter Harbour. But on that day in August with Margaret Oldenburg, Banks Island was entirely fogged in, so they couldn't land as planned. Flying farther east, they crossed onto Victoria at the western edge of Peel Point and continued straight on to land on what they named Oldenburg Lake.

For navigating in this area, Captain Boffa used a sheet of the new geological map (which blew out of the plane at Holman on their return trip), and found that it checked well with what they saw, except that the width of the point between Holman Island Post and Minto Inlet did not seem to check with the time required to fly across it.

About her lake, Miss Oldenburg wrote, "The lake was one of the largest, longer than it was wide, with a perfectly round island in the southern third of it. The island had steep sides and a flat top. There was some ice still in the lake, particularly at the northern end. We landed on the west bank at the south point of a sort of bay, into which a stream in a very rocky bed flowed. The coast directly south was of high, rounded, rose-colored rock. The men built a cairn on a shoulder there, in which they insisted I leave a note . . .

"In the bay the land sloped up more gradually to a ridge of another kind of rock (samples of each in the lichen collection). It rained about all the time we were there. A small bird or two — at a distance — was the only wildlife I saw. None of the terrain covered was favorable to footprints. Two hours collecting."

Taking off from Oldenburg Lake, Captain Boffa chose a curving course, avoiding heavy showers and fog, which took them to the coast of Dean's Dundas Bay and on to the base of Pemmican Point, thence west to Fort Collison. The building there had been torn down. Miss Oldenburg noted, "The vegetation seemed tropic compared with Melville. There were even willows over a foot high and a fern and paintbrush and hedysarum. Bear droppings but no tracks. A child's stocking indicated Eskimos had camped in the bay. Two hours collecting." Then they slept.

That day one of those small miracles of a lifetime occurred. The Eskimos came with Ernie's gas! They had taken 11 days from Holman Island Post in a rowboat with a single-cylinder outboard motor. The weather was bad and they had to take a roundabout route because of the ice, but they got it there in time to make

Captain Boffa happy. Arrangements were made a year ahead for such deliveries in those days!

There were still showers and fog when they took off again, but the Eskimos said they could get through, and they did. Holman Island Post had been fogged in from an hour or so after Boffa left until just a few hours before his return; there was still some ice in the harbor, but not enough to interfere with their landing.

The post manager told Margaret she had missed the peak of bloom by two weeks. But she found far more flowers during that visit than previously, so evidently it was a late season. She had two hours of collecting, guided by Father Bulliard, who had had some of the Eskimo people collect specimens before her arrival.

Boffa refueled there, then flew direct to Coppermine against a 15-mile-per-hour headwind, through weather so clear they could see the mainland coast all the way.

Concluding her report, Miss Oldenburg wrote, "I want to say that the flight was possible only by the kindness and good organization of Canadian Pacific Airlines, under Mr. Grant McConachie, Mr. May and Mr. Sturton, who did all they could, more especially

Pilot Boffa and mechanic De Blocq pose in the doorway of **Barkley Grow** *while Oldenburg collects specimens.*

in picking Captain Boffa for the trip and giving him a free hand to make the flight as he saw best; and in giving him a twin-engine plane for the trip. The mechanic of their choice was also very good. I also owe thanks to American Metals Ltd., who released Captain Boffa for the flight and helped with supplies, and to all the posts and wireless stations who helped with weather and other reports. The list of plants, lichens and rocks will be supplied by the University of Minnesota Herbarium.''

The following summer, 1946, Miss Oldenburg was in the Northwest Territories from late June, when she arrived at Fort Smith, to early October, when she finished pressing and drying some 2,886 sheets of specimens gathered on her travels. Her charter, with Ernie, was August 9 to 22, this time in the Norseman with mechanic Len De Blocq, whose pictures illustrate this chapter. They flew more than thirty seven hundred miles and got into Franklin expedition country again, as well as to Eskimo camps and northern missions never before visited by a white woman.

Leaving Yellowknife one Friday evening about supper time, in CF-BHV, they flew first to Fort Reliance, dropping down for gas, then to Carter Lake for an overnight stop in a trapper's line cabin.

First stop on the Oldenburg flight of '46 was Carter Lake, where a smooth shoreline made easy landing for the Norseman. (Len De Blocq)

Next day they went on to Thelon River and Baker Lake, where Captain Boffa welcomed an unexpected gas cache and Margaret Oldenburg was welcomed by Mrs. Hamilton, wife of the RCMP officer stationed there. (She hadn't seen another white woman in two years.) With their seven-year-old daughter, the Hamiltons were looking forward to a southern posting after living at Craig Harbour, Pangnirtung and other isolated places. That evening Margaret was

Repulse Lake provided quiet moorage when headwinds prevented the delivery of mail and food to nearby Repulse Bay. (Len De Blocq)

admiring the gorgeous magenta bloom of arctic fireweed growing along the shores of Baker Lake, while semi-tame ptarmigan wandered about the community. At that time the town boasted the RCMP detachment, Hudson's Bay post, Anglican and Roman Catholic missions, Royal Canadian Signals station, an airport under construction, and a number of RCAF personnel. One of them was helping the priest repair the outboard on his canoe when Margaret came by and found herself hailed by the missionary. He recognized her as the woman he had met at Dorset, a thousand miles away, seven years before.

From Baker Lake they flew on to Chesterfield Inlet for more gas, and picked up mail for Repulse Bay during a brief stop. At Repulse the tide was 12 feet high, with a headwind and rocky shore, not an inviting combination. So Ernie flew inland to a quiet lake for a safe night's mooring. Headwinds continued in the morning, which gave the botanist a chance to collect before they went back to Repulse to deliver the mail and some very welcome fresh vegetables from Yellowknife.

Friends of the two missionaries, Father Didier and Father Henri, had sent a small paper sack of potatoes from Chesterfield along with Boffa, because Repulse had been on short rations for many months. The supply boat had not reached them the year before because of bad ice and weather conditions. They had white whales, but little else, no fuel and no lights. They were expecting the supply schooner that week, and there was no ice in the way. Father Henri was convalescing at Repulse, although he was usually stationed at Pelly Bay. It was with him that De Poncins had stayed while he wrote his famous book *Kabloona,* and the priest told Miss Oldenburg how much he had admired the Belgian writer.

At Repulse, Margaret heard of whalebone houses built many

years before, but had no time to travel out to see them. They did learn the exact location of the mission at Pelly Bay, which was helpful, because shorelines in that area were frequently shown as dotted lines on Ernie's maps.

Committee Bay was piled high with ice, and fog forced Ernie to land the Norseman on a small inland lake, which they named, naturally, Fog Lake. The next morning they made a short hop to Committee Lake — not on Ernie's map (the Chantry Inlet sheet, Air Navigation edition), but as Margaret wrote, "Just west of the 'L' in Lake Ellice; a large lake, irregular in shape; we found shelter in a little bay . . . boxed by fog."

The next morning at a quarter past four, Ernie found a narrow corridor through the fog and they reached the base of Pelly Bay, after paralleling the north shore of Kellett River to find the coast, locating an Eskimo camp there, then following the shore to find the mission, "which is on a river unmarked on the map." Built of small stones, the mission itself blended perfectly into the stony background.

The tide was very high and they had to anchor the plane well out. Father Van der Velde greeted them, with several Eskimo families. They seemed well, despite the tough winter when most of their dogs had died. Because there had been so little trapping, Father Van der Velde had imported some walrus tusks and started the men carving with only a carpenter's rasp and a small, flat file for tools. Somehow, without instruction, these Pelly Bay Eskimos produced religious statues, scenes of native life, miniature bows and arrows, seal camps, igloos and fish. One purely imaginary figure of an angel intrigued Margaret Oldenburg; the carver had

The Pelly Bay mission house blends into its stony background.
Eskimo children here had never before seen a white woman.
(Len De Blocq)

94

never seen a picture of an angel, and the piece was, she wrote, "a bit like Italian primitives; how did he imagine the right folds in in the robe?" Father Van der Velde said those who could do the religious statues could not do the Eskimo scenes, and vice versa.

That morning in August 1946 there was a breakfast party at Pelly Bay mission. The visitors had brought eggs from Yellowknife, the first the Oblate Father had tasted since February 1943. Before he touched this special treat, he insisted on cooking some fresh arctic char for his guests. He tried to serve them a few leaves of lettuce from his cold frame box, but they felt he deserved them more than they did.

The people there ate the arctic sorrel, Father Van der Velde used fresh dandelion leaves for spring salad, and the Eskimos extended their scanty tobacco supplies with dried cranberry leaves. Thule relics from old stone houses to the north of the mission were shown later to Dr. Leechman of the National Museum of Canada, and some were kept for display there.

Father Van der Velde had a number of small children in his schoolroom, and Margaret Oldenburg was the first white woman they had ever seen. She, in turn, was seeing for the first time the type of parka worn by the women: short in front, long tail in back, pouch hood and unusual decorations.

When the fog lifted later that night, CF-BHV took off for Gjoa Havn, carrying a parcel to mail to the Van der Velde family back in Belgium; one of the finest ivory carvings, a replica of an Eskimo camp in complete detail. The previous winter the priest had received his first letter from home since the beginning of the war in 1939, and he was thrilled to have the chance to start some mail on its way back to them. The Norseman was the second plane ever to land at Pelly Bay Mission; Father Schultz, known as the Flying Priest of the Arctic, had dropped in once. Having three visitors was a great occasion!

Back out over the ice they flew and found a little bay at Gjoa Havn ice free for their landing, just before eleven. Captain Boffa sketched in some of the rivers they had seen en route, in addition to the Murchison, and sent them to the Canadian Hydrographic and Map Service for copying.

An hour's flight through warm, sunny skies the next afternoon brought BHV to the Blenkey Islands. There they looked for some evidence to support the story of a cache and a wreck told by some Eskimos to Major Burwash, who did a lot of northern surveying. They found nothing but three Eskimos graves. Rae Strait between King William and Boothia was shallow and ice free, but over deep water north of James Ross Strait was solid ice, so BHV flew inland

over Boothia to where the magnetic pole was marked on the map. Captain Boffa circled the plane over the pole, and the needle of the compass went around with the plane; it would not stay in any position. The needle of Ernie's pocket compass tried to stand on its head, Margaret reported.

South they flew until they found a lake on which to land for an hour's collecting, then on to Port Parry, at the mouth of a river where some Eskimos had fish nets down and a camp upriver. Only a few women and children, wearing ragged old fur clothing, were in camp. They knew no English other than "Patsy Klengenberg," the name of a trader along the coast. Margaret got the impression

"This is what the Arctic Ocean looks like in August," said photographer-mechanic De Blocq. "It's called open water."
(Len De Blocq)

they were getting plenty of fish, and the men were away sealing. A picnic developed with hardtack, corned beef, butter and jam for one and all, and American cigarettes for the women in the group — who offered some back to Margaret after lunch, from her own supply.

On they went that evening from Port Parry to Gjoa Havn where they found the Bay post locked up and empty except for bales of fur in the warehouse. Here Ernie and Len spent their time repairing

Boffa and Oldenburg shared corned beef, biscuits and cigarettes, if not language, with women and children near Port Parry. (Len De Blocq)

a hole in one pontoon, punched through by a rocky beach when they had landed on one of the Blenkey Islands. Ernie ran the plane up onto an inverted dog sled for a workbench, and they soon had it repaired.

West they flew the next afternoon, finding lots of ice blocking the channel at Cape Seaforth, but found a prosperous Eskimo camp at the head of a sheltered bay. Here they picked up one of the men, hoping he could guide them to some caves reported nearby. Ernie was amazed to find that this native, who had never flown before, knew where he was all the time during the 20-minute flight. He showed them a small unoccupied shack and a cairn, which he said were made by *kabloonas*. Margaret heard later from Hudson's Bay men that they had built it there. Dropping off their guide, they flew over to Chantrey Inlet that evening, then up to the mouth of Back River, where they had arranged for a gas cache. But a thorough search turned up no familiar aviation gas barrels; that wasn't a good omen.

Finally Ernie flew inland to Franklin Lake, looking for a safe landing in the dark on a strange, rocky shore, where they spent the night. Now short of gas, BHV headed back to Perry River in the morning, and finally located the post some 10 miles away from its mapped location. The post manager was at Cambridge Bay, but they were able to refuel. There were heavy rainstorms inland, and considerable ice to the north, so Captain Boffa turned the

Norseman back to "civilization" at Cambridge Bay, where they landed about eight o'clock.

Here they found other visitors, including Inspector Learmonth of the Bay. There were two or three Eskimo schooners in the harbor, which meant fresh seal liver for supper, cooked by Mrs. Scotty Gall, wife of the Bay manager at Cambridge. They were still waiting for the annual supply ship to come, making do with what they had, and the native people were waiting for supplies before they could get away to their sealing and fishing. At two o'clock in the morning, Margaret was enjoying a hot tub in Isabel Gall's kitchen and enjoying a reunion with her old friend, who thoughtfully pulled down the blinds to keep out the light!

There were several sick people at Cambridge, and in her report Margaret wrote, "One woman had a breast nearly eaten away by some sore. I don't know whether she was the one whose husband took her away so she couldn't be sent out, because their small son would have had to go with her and he didn't want his son to go. The police and Bay boats had refused to take any sick people. The HBC had warned their staff not to ask for mercy flights and the police were afraid of being dismissed if they asked for one.

"The only patient I saw was a boy with a badly swollen abdomen, getting worse all the time. No one there had ever seen such a case and did not know what to do for him; their telegram to Aklavik [where there was a doctor and hospital] had not been acknowledged. It was obvious that the boy would die if left there, so with the pilot's consent I asked the police to O.K. my doing something about it. By dint of much telegraphing we arranged for the RCAF *Canso,* which was coming in, to take him to Coppermine and said we would fly him south from there. It happened to be at the same time as the trial at Coppermine; two doctors there diagnosed the boy's sickness as tuberculosis of the bowels and tapped him, releasing three quarts of fluid. The captain of the RCMP boat *St. Roche* at first refused to take him on to Tuktoyaktuk, but relented and took him, along with a child who had tuberculosis of the spine, and the child's mother to look after her.

"I do not blame the boats for not wanting to take sick people," Miss Oldenburg wrote. "They have little accommodation for them, and even after the patients get to Tuk they have to lie around for days or weeks before getting to Aklavik; not an efficient or satisfactory state of affairs, but the only possiblity when no one will order a plane unless the natives can pay for it. While I was in Yellowknife, a flight was made to bring in Patsy Klengenberg's adopted son, badly burned in the loss of the schooner *Aklavik.* After a stay at the Con [mine] hospital he was flown out to Edmonton . . . and

at last reports was doing better than expected. As 50 percent of his body was burned, this was a very serious case. [Klengenberg, an Eskimo trader, could pay for the plane.]

"If there were a hospital at Coppermine," the botanist reported, "more of the natives from Cambridge and farther east would get medical attention. It would overcome their reluctance at going so far from home as Aklavik or Edmonton; also, all the native schooners from the east go to Coppermine and so there is assured transportation during the boat season. Tuberculosis is getting much more prevalent in this district [to judge by health and death reports on Eskimos I know there] and from what I have seen and learned from the nurses, the hospitals in NWT aren't able to give adequate sanitarium services, which are really a necessity for serious, long-term TB cases."

After an overnight stop at Washburn Lake on Holman Island, which still had a sheet of ice on one bay, they flew the four hundred miles to Holman Island Post, where they met Father Franche and his mission ship, *Lady of Lourdes*. Paris born and bred, Father Franche had been in the Canadian north since his first years as a missionary and was known as one of the best "ice men" in the Arctic. Traveling back and forth across the top of the world in his sturdy little ship, calling in at isolated missions regularly, he held the record for the trip from Tuk to Holman via Coppermine, more than seven hundred miles of ocean travel in four days.

Short on gas, Boffa sat down for a night on Franklin Lake. He and De Blocq built the cairn around an empty gas drum. (Len De Blocq)

The *Lady of Lourdes* had just figured in the rescue of an RCAF Norseman crew after the plane had sunk in the Holman Island harbor. (The *Lady of Lourdes* is now a National Historic Site, beached at Tuktoyaktuk near the Roman Catholic mission.)

The sea was too rough for landing in Johnson Bay that night, so Ernie went on to Investigator Lake, four miles upriver from the bay. There they saw fresh musk ox tracks. En route to Mercy Bay the next morning, August 20, fog cut off much of the view to the north and east, and the rivers were not as shown on the map. Margaret notes succinctly, "Captain Boffa's comments on this were sent direct to Mr. Max G. Cameron of the Hydrographic and Map Service." Mercy Bay was frozen solid, and they did not fly over the ice, so they missed seeing the remains, if any, of the old ship, the *Investigator,* abandoned there.

Landing well up the bay on the west side, they saw a herd of 5 white caribou running off, and at intervals during the day's flying, other groups from 2 to 13, all white. On the beach they found three pieces of driftwood, obviously from a ship, which Ernie was positive came from McClure's *Investigator,* abandoned nearby in 1853.

Flying from there to Caribou Lake, BHV joined a flock of some three hundred wild geese. After a quick gas stop at Walker Bay,

Trader Patsy Klengenberg's schooner Aklavik, *here frozen in near Wilmot Island, later burned in Cambridge Bay.*

they returned to Holman Island Post and a night's rest at Father Bulliard's mission. Then it was back to Coppermine, where Miss Oldenburg stayed with her Anglican mission friends, Canon Harold and Edie Webster, for her fifth annual visit. Here McLean, the wireless operator, lent his new canoe and outboard motor so Margaret could be taken upriver to the hills near Bloody Falls, scene of an ancient massacre of Indians by Eskimos. She found unusual growth in the protected valley; for example, there was a willow about 18 feet high. Natives were fishing in the river for food because the caribou had failed them inland that year.

The next day, bringing Bishop Trocellier and Vince Kost out with

The Norseman CPR waits at Tuktoyaktuk, often called Tuk Tuk or just Tuk, near the western edge of the Canadian Arctic.

them, BHV's party flew to Cameron Bay for gas, to Fort Rae to drop off the bishop, and then home to Yellowknife in time for supper. Despite her huge bags of collected specimens, Margaret Oldenburg just ran her strong brown hands through her short-cropped hair, lit another cigarette, and said, "Me? I just go along for the ride."

There was certainly more to it than that, or Captain Boffa wouldn't have been bothered with her. She was an intelligent, well-read, arctic history buff, as well as botanist. Her botanical collecting qualified her to enter Canada as a "scientific expedition" and get to places no one else ever saw in those days. She had three degrees: one from Vassar, one from the University of Minnesota and one in library science. She had been a teacher and a university librarian.

Walker Bay was scheduled as a gas cache stop for Oldenburg and Boffa on their 1945 trip, but the gas wasn't there.

In her 15 years of northern travels, she had become a friend of nearly every Hudson's Bay family across the Northwest Territories' coast. Years later, she was still sending them good new books about the north at Christmas. She made her last flight with Ernie Boffa in 1954, to Holman, Banks Island, Bridport Inlet, across Victoria Island to Minto Inlet, then south again.

Since she had been traveling into the Arctic during World War II, I asked her once in an interview whether she was really a Russian spy, which sent her off into gales of choking laughter mixed with cigarette smoke. She kept up a fascinating correspondence with missionaries and traders through the Arctic for years and was an encyclopedia of northern information. She sent gifts back to all who were helpful or hospitable — something unusual for northern hosts whose homes served as hotels or restaurants in those times — and went to considerable trouble to make the gift something especially meaningful to each recipient.

She would gladly talk about her forays into the Arctic, and she enjoyed telling how each expedition went, but there was little, if any, mention of herself. That was probably why Ernie Boffa enjoyed taking her along. She talked little because of her deafness, traveled light, and was always ready to go when he was. Margaret Oldenburg was unique in the North.

— 10 —
UPS AND DOWNS

In 1950, after freezeup, Ernie took a leave of absence from CPAir to join Yellowknife Airways, in which he had a 20 percent interest with owner Matt Berry, who had bought CPAir's bush flying business. Ernie had the option of going back to CPAir whenever he wanted to, which was nice. He and Matt didn't always see eye to eye in their business deals, but they went along until one disaster after another finished them. Dennison cracked up, killing Bulmer; Johnny Bourassa was lost with the Stinson; Mush Sharon drowned; Doug Ireland cracked up the Bellanca. As if those problems weren't bad enough, the competition over at Associated had a habit of reporting every small infraction to the Department of Transport — overloading, for example — and Ernie still hotly states, "They were overloading worse than us!"

In this 1950 photo, Don Thompson of CPAir chats with Boffa, on leave to fly for Yellowknife Airways, part of which he owns. (David West)

In EFI, a Piper Supercruiser, Boffa could "land on a lily pad." Out looking for oil near Great Slave Lake, he carried the pole ramp so he could get ashore more easily on small-lake landings.

The last straw came for Boffa when he got the company to buy one new plane — in fact he financed it himself — a Beaver. They had one at Fort Smith and Ernie wanted one at Yellowknife to compete for the government business. But instead of getting to fly it himself, Boffa found that the new plane had been sent down on another oil contract, so was not available to fly the Northwest Territories' government people around on official trips. Boffa was disgusted. Anyway, Berry sold out to Associated. Boffa stayed with them for about a month, then went back to CPAir.

The winter of 1951-52 saw the Boffas based in Vancouver, with E.J.B. training as an airline pilot, flying on the right-hand side on routes such as Vancouver to the Queen Charlotte Islands, Prince Rupert, and Calgary.

"We flew direct to Rupert three times a week in fog and rain. It wasn't my kind of flying. I knew I didn't want to be checked out as a captain if it meant that type of flying, and I wanted to go back where I belonged, the North. But I hated to leave because Grant McConachie was president, and his executive staff of CPAir were some of the fairest guys you could fly for."

About that time, John Anderson Thomson, mining engineer and the only resident Dominion land surveyor in the Territories, came down from Yellowknife to visit in Vancouver. He didn't find it too hard to talk Boffa into going back with him, at least as far as Edmonton. There Tommy Fox hired Ernie to go back to Yellowknife.

"So I drove back to Edmonton with John and I was supposed to go and fly with Johnny Nesbitt. He flew for Eldorado and the RCMP at the end of the war, and spent a lot of time in the Bush. Then, one day, when they made the Goldfields discovery of uranium, Johnny staked a bunch of claims and made it pretty big. Lebine took over those claims and started the Nesbitt-Lebine Mine.

"Well, I was supposed to be flying for them, but I went to Yellowknife and started flying for Associated again, and stayed with them until the summer of 1953."

That summer, uranium was "in style" in the North. Jake Woolgar, a former RCAF fighter pilot who had come to Yellowknife after the war and started a prospecting syndicate, asked Boffa to join him. That was right down Ernie's alley; he had always had a special interest in prospecting and hankered for a chance to get into it, so he agreed. Jake had an old four-place Fairchild 24.

Ernie was expert at making do with equipment he carried. Here, it's mug-up time so he melts snow to make tea. (Richard Harrington)

107

They went looking for uranium, and found several showings, but none which proved good enough to make deals on.

Toward fall they decided to go and have a look at some copper indications Ernie had seen while flying in the Arctic earlier, especially the one up the Tree River.

It was a very impressive sight from the air, a big quartz vein cutting dramatically across the river, the whole sheer cliff stained from copper. Jake, seeing it for the first time, could hardly wait until they had landed to get it staked.

"Since it was an original find for me," Ernie recalls, "Jake said we'll call the claims the Adam and Eve. But other than its spectacular looks, it turned out to be worthless. All that green stain was from a very small amount of chalcopyrite."

It was autumn, and Jake decided to wind up their prospecting for the season. But Ernie wasn't through, so he rented Associated Airway's Stinson and staked some claims in the Marion River country, north of Fort Rae. Hubie Giauque had made a good uranium find in that area, resulting in a good deal, and a rush followed. Claims were in demand, so Ernie was able to sell some to the Toronto promoters.

Then he teamed up with Len Peckham, a prospector he had grubstaked earlier.

"Rayrock Mines was doing some development work on its property in the Marion River area, so we concentrated our prospecting in that area, and sure enough, we made a find of

Boffa and Jake Woolgar camped on Lake Utuk to look at a promising copper deposit Boffa had spotted on Tree River.

A mechanic before he was a pilot, Boffa could and often did make his own repairs — an invaluable skill in bush flying. In the upper photo, taken in Yellowknife where Boffa had a private float, he works on the engine of CPAir's BTX.

uranium and got a deal in Toronto. Then we bought the Fairchild 24 from Jake and made plans for some more prospecting in the spring.

"But one day in January of 1954 I got a message from Grant McConachie to come down to Vancouver, there was somebody wanted to talk to me. Turned out to be the beginning of the DEW line." (The Distant Early Warning system was designed and built by the United States in northern Canada to detect any enemy aerial missiles or bombers from across the Arctic Ocean.)

The man he saw in Vancouver was O.E. Ludwig, project manager for both Western Electric Company in New York and Northern Construction Company in Canada. He and E.J.B. hit it off just

Boffa always carried sleeping bag, tent, sextant, shovel, flares, rifle, two weeks' food, and a Geiger counter. Here, at his float in Yellowknife, he readies the Fairchild for takeoff.

fine. At the time of that first interview, Ludwig was looking for a pilot who knew the Canadian Arctic well enough to be able to locate sites to be picked for radar stations on the DEW line. Grant McConachie knew Boffa was that man.

"They quizzed me about a lot of things," Ernie remembers. "They wanted suggestions about where they could bring in the Bristol Freighter and a tractor to plow a runway for the C24. I said they should start from Cambridge Bay in the east, because the facilities were already there."

Northern Construction had some aerial photos of the Canadian Arctic taken in the summer, and they needed equipment to build the first strip somewhere between the Alaska-Yukon border and Boothia Peninsula. But in wintertime in the Arctic, it is very difficult to locate a place that has been chosen on the map, because of the lack of distinguishing geographical features — everything is covered with snow, everything is white. There is so little contrast it is difficult to distinguish sea ice from snow-covered ground. They needed Boffa.

So Ernie began flying that winter for Northern Construction, using the CPAir Norseman. He headed up from Yellowknife to Paulatuk on the Yukon coast, because he had some gas cached there and there was some CPAir gas as well. He decided his starting point would be a bay at Pearce Point, where there was still an old building standing. This he chose as the main site for the western end of the operation. Cambridge was to be the main point for the eastern half.

He took along with him Andy Madore, a pilot and friend of many years. Andy had been an instructor at the Saskatoon Flying Club before the war, got a job when Trans Canada Airlines started in 1937, then joined the RCAF when war began and was later in charge of the Commonwealth Air Training School at Virden, Manitoba. When Ernie ran into him in Edmonton that winter, he was at loose ends and just the man Boffa was looking for. The two flew north, unloaded the first supplies at Pearce Point, then flew over to Coppermine, bought hand shovels from the Bay, and hired some Eskimos to come back and start shoveling a runway in the snow at Pearce Point. While that started, Boffa flew back to Yellowknife and brought back three good carpenters accustomed to working in the cold — and it was cold! For 10 days straight they worked at 50° below zero.

They proceeded to set up tent frames, and when the DC-3 landed with the first load of plywood and equipment, the handymen built the radio operator's shack and other shelters. Ernie also hired some local people in the area, some of whom stayed with the DEW line for years.

While the construction was going on, Boffa flew back to Yellowknife, picked up some more representatives from Western Electric and Northern Construction, and flew them back and forth along the white arctic coastline. From the air they chose Cape Parry as the first site location, rather than Pearce Point, and the camp was later moved over there. Then they flew east as far as Cambridge Bay, overnighting at Coppermine, and picked sites along Victoria Island. Boffa landed at these points later and flagged the sites for first landings by other crews. Learmonth of the Bay helped the expedition with his great collection of maps of eastern Boothia, and the organizing of supplies and much-needed equipment for the sites.

Boffa's title during this special assignment was technical adviser to Ludwig, the project manager. Ernie had the pleasure of being the first guy with power to sign for the DEW line in the North. His only troublesome purchase was a case of rum he bought for the men building the shelters and shoveling the runway of concrete-hard, drifted snow at Pearce Point at 50° below zero.

"We never abused it," Ernie says indignantly, "but we used it to make hot rums for those men and it kept everybody happy. I put it on my expense account and I had more trouble with that one item than anything else for months afterward. 'We can't pay for rum,' they said. 'Call it something else — these vouchers have to be approved in Washington!' 'I can't do that,' I said, 'I'm not going to lie about it.' The accounting office wanted me to call it antifreeze! This went on until spring, when I was in the Edmonton office on business one day and I said, 'Well, Mr. Ludwig, what about that expense account?' The head of Western Electric, who was there from New York, exploded. 'Pay the man!' he shouted. 'It doesn't matter what it's listed as; I'll see that it gets paid. Boffa is right. It's not exactly Florida up there! We've still got a lot to learn about working in the Arctic!' And that was the end of that."

In those first few weeks, as everything waited to roll, it was Boffa who started them rolling. Dan McIvor came up from British Columbia, where he had rigged up the first water bombers to fight forest fires. He flew the Beaver from Pacific Western Airways. He had a young man with him who joined Boffa on a flight out of

DEW line site selection required a pilot who knew the Arctic as Boffa did. Here his Norseman sits out bad weather near Eldorado.

112

Pearce Point one day. They cut across country to Eldorado, ran into some stinking weather, and used a lot of gas. Boffa finally set the plane down south of Bluenose Lake, west of Dismal Lakes, to sit out the weather, and built an igloo for the night. They were there for two nights before the storm cleared and Ernie was able to get a shot with his sextant at the stars. Short of gas, he still figured they could make it to Coppermine the next day, and they did. He filled the tank there and went back to Yellowknife.

Jim Hunt, Northern Construction's superintendent of the west portion of the DEW line, arrived so Ernie flew him to Cape Parry, and ran into "one hell of a headwind" in an arctic storm. He picked up what he figured was the Horton River and followed it, and kept on following it, figuring there was nothing else he could do until they flew out of the storm or found a good spot to land. About 15 miles from the mouth of the river, low on gas but sure of his location, Boffa sat her down on the river near a nice spot with some small spruce trees for shelter.

"Well, I set up a camp for them there, in the bitter cold, the wind blowing like hell, and these guys just stood around until I got the tent up for them with the heater going. I cut spruce boughs and made them comfortable in there, which was a good thing, because we were there for three nights. I was in radio contact with the camp at Cape Parry and they knew where we were. I asked them to talk to any aircraft in the region and tell them to drop us some gas. The wind quit finally, but nobody dropped us any fuel until McIvor flew in with some. I knew I could have taken a chance on the amount of gas I had left, and flown to camp alone, but I couldn't very well leave those guys on their own."

After that it was a matter of clearing runways and setting up tent camps. A Cat (tractor) train operator named Gessi, from Circle, Alaska, traveled across country, down the Blow River with some monstrous equipment; D8 Cats, huge trucks, lowboys, everything was hauled overland. Joe Kelly was the train boss. He later became a photographer in Anchorage, according to Ernie. These men plowed the runways for the C124 to fly in the freight, and the western crew kept well ahead of the eastern DEW line workers.

When spring came all the sites had been established. Boffa had to leave the DEW line job, because he had a contract to fly in and do some contract drilling on some claims, so he went back with his partner, Len Peckham, as arranged. He bought a new Cessna and returned to the DEW line in the fall of 1954, flying under contract for the winter.

Ernie tells one of the things he remembers about Tuktoyaktuk (which figures prominently nearly 40 years later as the center of gas and oil exploration in the Beaufort): "At Tuk we rented this little Cat to come up and try to make a runway, but it couldn't do much, the drifts were packed so hard. It looked pretty good from the air, but the drifts were a foot and a half deep. If you broke through, they would stop you — right now! So what I did, I went over the hill from Tuk and found a nice lake.

"That was a nice, smooth runway, almost glare ice, and I marked it out for the Bristol to come in. Well, the Bristol came along, with a D4 on board, and the pilot saw this nice smooth-looking runway at Tuk and brought her down there. Hit that snow and went OOMPH! and he couldn't move an inch after that. He'd have had one hell of a time digging out of there by hand, but he hadn't been there more than an hour when, by golly, around the corner comes Gessi with a D8 Cat! How lucky can you get? They plowed him out and away he went.

"Over at Terror Bay, west of Gjoa Havn, we had the same trouble with deep snow on the runway. It was terrible for landing. They told me to go and do something about it. So I went over there. The snow was worse than at Tuk, deep and drifted and hard as rock. It would have wiped out the undercarriage of a Bristol. So I went up on a hill and had a look around, and there's a nice lake back there, so I marked out a runway. The Bristol came in the same day — safely. That's the kind of thing I was there for."

Boffa left again in the spring of 1955 and was back in the fall for his third winter, this time with a Beaver he had leased. But Federal Electric was starting to take over from the original contractors. He didn't like the new setup as much, so he got out. It had been a good experience.

"Ludwig was good to me," says Ernie. "He appreciated what I did that first winter. When the project was completed, he went to Iran to build dams and airstrips there, and he sent me a round-the-world jet ticket to go to Iran on the excuse that he wanted me to advise them on their flying requirements. I never took advantage of it, too busy with other things.

"There were a lot of interesting things at the time, which meant nothing special to me just then, but now, when I look back, I'm kind of proud of some of that stuff. It's hard to believe that I went through so many things. A lot of important things did happen in those days — and all of it is true."

— 11 —
THE MEMORY MACHINE

Talking to Boffa, it doesn't really matter what subject one begins, the conversation always ends up with a short story about flying, or planes, or the people who flew them. His head is full of mental snapshots, filed through the years, so the mention of a name, or a date, or an aircraft type will push the button to unlock the file and the details pop up, as fresh and as colorful as on the day they happened.

Today, in the news, we read that an old Fox Moth, flown into a lake near Yellowknife by Gordon Wonnacott 30 years ago, is to be recovered, refurbished for some $40,000, and set up as a special exhibit at the Prince of Wales Heritage Centre in the Northwest Territories capitol. The name Fox Moth is the key to a special file and out come the memories . . .

On January 22, 1949, Max Ward's Fox Moth set off from Yellowknife on a routine flight with pilot Grant Ford, carrying Con Mine geologist Henry Dennis and a company prospector. They were never seen alive again. When the plane's return was overdue, and a routine search turned up nothing, local pilots conducted their own search for two days, then called in the RCAF Search and Rescue team. Many miles were covered and hours of strain endured before the burned remnants were spotted February 1 by Fred Riley, flying with Vern Simmonds. All three men were dead. At the funeral several days later, Boffa and other bush pilots flew low in a final salute.

The code word "smuggling" brings out the Lethbridge file. When E.J.B. was flying with the barnstorming group, with an occasional trip to Great Falls, he came under surveillance by the RCMP because they were watching for someone who was smuggling by air. Every few days they would come by and ask to check Ernie's logbook. Ernie got annoyed about that and went downtown to see the inspector.

"I asked them what was going on, and said, 'I'm not doing any smuggling! Tell your men to get off my back!' The guy was very decent and kept his word, and they didn't bother me anymore."

If the code word is "caribou," that leads to stories about flying

115

the caribou survey in the Barren Lands one spring for Dr. John Kelsall, a federal mammalogist. Ernie flew the Cessna, and Smoky Hornby the Piper Super Cub, rounding up calves like flying cowboys.

In his report, *The Migratory Barren-Ground Caribou of Canada,* published by the Queen's printer in 1968 for the Department of Indian Affairs and Northern Development, John Kelsall wrote, "A special debt is owed to the bush pilots who participated in the enormous amount of flying called for in our work. Some provided many hours of flying gratis, and gave regular and careful reports of caribou sightings. In order to carry out investigations at all seasons, in unmapped and remote country, a number of pilots did considerably more than could be expected as a commercial endeavor. A complete roster of these men is not possible. However, because of their long association with the project and particular helpfulness to the author, individual appreciation is extended to the following Yellowknife pilots: Ernie Boffa, Dave Floyd, the late Al Shankoff, Smoky Hornby and the late Ken Stockall."

Try another name on that memory machine: Hank Koenen. A ferry pilot during the war, he came from the Edmonton area, and then flew DC-3s for Alf Caywood of Eldorado. At Yellowknife he got together with a pilot from eastern Canada, George Pigeon, but after a while Hank went on his own, and stayed a loner.

As Ernie says, "He wasn't interested in being the most famous pilot in the North, or the busiest; he just did it his own way. He ran a real good one-man operation, and that's a pretty good way to do it. If you get a little too big, well, then you're in trouble. It doesn't pay in between, until you get to be a big airline. So Hank just kept it to the size he could handle and did it his own way. He was a real nice guy to have around, always ready to help if you needed something. He finally sold out when he got tired of flying all the time, and moved to Edmonton. But he's always got something going — sort of like a horse trader. Nice guy, Hank."

Say Father Adam to Ernie, and back comes the memory. In 1944, Father Adam was the Oblate priest at Bathurst Inlet. The word came to Yellowknife that he was very sick and needed medical attention. Ernie went up to get him, together with mechanic Ed Young and Father Gathy. It was the middle of winter with the worst possible flying conditions. To go from Yellowknife via Coppermine was the safe route, but it would take longer. To do it fast, Boffa decided to cut across the territory, but that meant extra gas supplies had to be on board.

They loaded extra 45-gallon drums into the cabin of the Norseman, filtered the gas into the drums, and fitted a wobble

116

pump with a hose out of the cabin, up to the wing and into the tank, and then went nonstop from Yellowknife to Bathurst Inlet. It was a great feat at the time. Now, nearly 40 years later, there are scheduled runs between all those places with the magic names.

And speaking of Oblate fathers, there was a Radiosonde operator at Coppermine in those early days, Cupie, who called everybody "Mo." Thus, Father Lapointe was Father Moe; Father Lamere was Father Lamoe and Father Delalonde became Father Delamoe. Ernie still laughs about that.

There are stories about Anglican missionaries as well, including the late Bishop Barfoot, who was a passenger with Ernie from Boothia to Aklavik, visiting all the Anglican missions in the western Arctic. They got in some good bridge games on that trip. At Reid Island, Billy Joss, who loved to play bridge, was a loser, and not a happy one. In the middle of the night he came out and woke Boffa up triumphantly. "You didn't win that game," Billy shouted. "You forgot my honors!"

Archdeacon Harold Webster was another one who was a keen bridge player. Ernie likes to tell about this episode. "In 1951, 'Webbie,' a canon at the time, was in Yellowknife with an Eskimo and I flew them and Smoky Hornby as crewman back to Coppermine, where Webbie was based at the Anglican mission. We got as far as the Coppermine mountains and the weather was so bad I had to land at Dismal Lakes, where the small cabin American Metals built still remained.

"The wind was really blowing and it was a good 40° below. While I tied the Norseman down, Smoky chopped up the old dock and we lit a fire in the shack.

"After warming up we ate and then Webbie pulled out a deck of cards and asked, 'How about a game of bridge?'

"I looked at the Eskimo, who couldn't speak English, and said to Webbie, 'Can he play?' Webbie said, 'No, but we'll teach him.' We cut the cards and it was Webbie and the Eskimo versus Smoky and me.

"Boy, what a game of bridge! Webbie could speak Inuit and did everything but swear at his partner, when he didn't play the cards expected of him. The poor guy couldn't speak English and sure as hell had never played a card game before.

"We didn't have a lantern, or candles, so I made a bitch lamp out of an empty sardine tin, some string twisted together, and some melted butter for fuel. It smelled just like a dairy in that shack. Smoky called it 'The Great Dismal Lake Arctic Dairy Bridge Tournament.'

"Harold Webster was my kind of missionary. His priority was

first the health of the natives, then their souls. At least that's the way I felt about him. He did a lot of doctoring up there, including 'kitchen' dentistry. Webbie had my greatest respect and remains forever a good friend of my family. When he officiated at my daughter Kay's wedding to Smoky, he could count on one hand the number of white weddings that he had conducted.

"There were some other missionary priests of the Catholic Church that were like Webster and also had my respect. Namely, Fathers Lamere, Lapointe, Gathy, and one that was at Paulatuk, but I've forgotten his name."

Another Coppermine name which still triggers a memory almost daily at the Boffa home in Westwood, Los Angeles, is Walt Taylor. He was supposed to send the weather reports by radio each morning, south from Coppermine, but he was a very hard man to wake up out of a sound sleep. He had two alarm clocks, but even they didn't do it. So Walt put them in a metal tub, or a dish pan, to make them louder when the alarm went off, right beside his ear. Even then he sometimes slept through all the racket.

So now, when Ernie looks in his Los Angeles morning paper for the Canadian weather report, and it's missing, as frequently happens, he just says to Nettie, "Walt is sleeping in again!" And she knows what he means.

Say Washburn and the stories begin again. One of them would be about Minto Inlet on Victoria Island, where Boffa later took sport fishermen from the lodge on Great Bear Lake to catch char at the mouth of the river. But, years before, with Linc and Tahoe Washburn, and Father Bulliard as interpreter, they had flown in there to an Eskimo settlement at the mouth of the river. There was a little mission on an island which Bulliard served.

Here, a very old couple claimed to know where a great mass of copper could be found. They had gone up there, years before, when they were first married, into a deep valley, following up the river, where there was a lot of broken rock, the same kind of formation as at Coppermine. So, with the Washburns and the old Eskimo, Boffa flew up the valley, landing as close as he could get, but they still had to walk 15 miles to the spot the Eskimo remembered — and didn't find it.

But a year later, one of the natives came in with a Keen's Mustard tin in which were notes recording the staking of that pioneer copper claim. The date early in the century; the staker was an Irishman who had come into the area with a whaling ship. Trader Billy Calder gave it to E.J.B., who got Kennecott Copper interested enough to charter the Beaver, find the Eskimo who had brought in the can, and go exploring again. They found a rock cairn marking the old claim, and there was some significant native copper, including some huge chunks on the surface. But nobody ever went further.

These bits and pieces of mineral finds always excited Ernie, who rarely completed a flight in the North without spotting something interesting he wanted to get back to. He had no formal training as a prospector, but he was a quick learner and he read as much as he could get his hands on, listened to the men he worked with, and in later years was in charge of prospecting parties for local syndicates run by Yellowknifers such as Jimmy Mason and Len White.

If you say gold rush to Boffa, it's not the Klondike you hear about, but the Firth River gold rush in Yukon Territory in 1947-48. He took the first plane into that one and marked out the first runway, then other aircraft flew in with staking parties, among them Mike Zupko from Aklavik and Jim Keir for Imperial Oil. One of the prized possessions in the Boffa home in Los Angeles is an oil painting by geologist Marvin Mangus, showing Boffa's plane in

Now in Los Angeles, Nettie and Ernie live with mementoes of earlier times in colder climes. The painting shows a staking camp and Ernie's plane on Firth River, northern Yukon Territory. (Jim Whyard)

the snow and the tent camp nearby, at Firth River. The gold turned out to be thin flakes and the flurry died down soon afterward.

Say TB Survey and you get an earful of modern arctic medical history. Ernie had been flying federal health people around the Arctic, and had often picked up Eskimos with tuberculosis who had to be flown south for treatment at the Charles Camsell Hospital in Edmonton. But it was in 1949 that he flew Dr. John Callaghan with the first x-ray clinic to cover the western Arctic, from Pelly Bay to Aklavik. It was the first time in the history of the Arctic that such a thorough medical examination of the Eskimo people had been done.

Ernie says, "I don't think we missed very many — just the few who were inland and couldn't get to the posts while we were there. And wherever we went, everyone was pressed into service. Hudson's Bay men filled out cards, mechanics looked after the x-ray machine, even the RCAF boys who were at Cambridge Bay had to help. We covered a thousand miles of coast. It was that same year that the influenza bug was brought in from Outside and many of those people died. We were flying doctors and nurses back up to those same settlements later."

Mention Perry River Eskimos, and Ernie remembers Angulalik, an Eskimo, the only one to run a Hudson's Bay trading post at that time. He had little or no education or training, and would order "12 ——— Made in Japan," whatever was on the outside of the packing cases, but E.J.B. remembers him as "a gentleman among the Eskimos."

The words musk ox summon a snapshot from Ernie's memory, flying near Bathurst when he spotted a herd below and circled for a few moments to watch the hairy beasts. When the plane flew overhead, they all ran up the slope of a hill, except two bulls, which began to fight. Boffa thinks the noise of the plane angered them and they took it out on each other. But what he remembers vividly is that they would run at each other broadside, in full attack, horns lowered, and at the last second the one standing his ground would turn his head and meet his opponent in a resounding crash, taking the full thrust with his powerful neck.

Musk ox also recalls the skulls of those animals, scattered on the rocky outcrop near Oldenburg Lake, which they used to hold down the tent.

Say Don Cameron and Ernie's eyes twinkle, and out come the stories about this great prospector for Frobisher.

Boffa was flying the big Bellanca, CF-BTW, for CPAir, servicing American Metals, flying to Eldorado and hauling supplies for Cameron. But when he came in with a Norseman one day to Cameron's camp, he was asked "What are you doing with this airplane? I like that panty-legged one. It's a good Protestant airplane!"

Mention Dick Laidman, and the computer-mind brings up the story about flying freighter canoes with the Norseman, on skis, when Dick was mechanic at the Yellowknife base. They built an outrigger device, took the Norseman's door off, tied on the canoes, and took off. It worked, but it was damned cold!

Ask about Danny Bagan, one of the colorful Yellowknife

The Bellanca BTW, a big clunker to Boffa, was known in Cameron's camp as "panty-legged, a good Protestant plane."

prospectors, and Ernie conjures up the picture of the Irishman setting up camp at Indian Lake, when they went in to recover a CPAir Norseman that had gone through the ice. Danny would haul a frozen quarter of beef onto a log, put his dirty moccasin on it, and cut off the steaks with a swede saw, then say, "Son-of-a-bitch good steak!"

Another familiar Yellowknife character in the staking boom days was George Midgeley, who, besides being a mining engineering type, was also a bit of a poet. He'd been on the Canol pipe line, then got in on the Yellowknife rush and was working for Claude Watt at Gordon Lake. Joe Harriman and Johnny Jacobsen were there, grubstaked by Herb Kerr and Boffa. Midgeley called Bertha Watt the "Duchess of Argonaut" (Argonaut was the name of their mining syndicate). Mrs. Harriman became "Lady Gordon" and Johnny was dubbed "the Baron of Handshake Bay."

Ask about miracles, and Boffa recalls a flight with Oldenburg in 1953, when they went east specifically to find the cabin on the Thelon River where the now legendary John Hornby and two other young Englishmen had died, back in the 1920s, of starvation. The three graves were there, with rocks and crosses marking their location, so Boffa straightened them up and did some repairs around the site. The roof had caved in on the historic cabin. Then they headed back. But the spring breakup of the river had washed their cache of gas away; that meant they would have to cut short their exploring and head for Yellowknife. Then, just as they were flying on, they spotted a drum of gasoline way up in the bushes, and landed. It was full of AV gas — one of theirs! Talk about an answer to a prayer!

Say arctic char, and Boffa automatically replies: "Tree River,

121

This scene on Wilmot Island was replayed often across the Canadian Arctic.

about one hundred miles east of Coppermine. There used to be a Hudson's Bay post there, with Scotty Gall and Billy Joss running it. That was a great place for char. The RCMP used to fish there for their winter's supply of dog food. When the lodge opened on Great Bear I used to fly the fishermen over there for a change of pace; they got exciting sport near the falls.''

Boffa flew for Great Bear Lodge from 1962-70, in the summers only, choosing the campsites and setting up cabins. The sport fishermen who flew up from the States used to love to go along with Boffa, who knew everything there was to know about that part of the Territories. For years Ernie was in demand to pilot visiting writers such as Grancel Fitz of *Field and Stream,* Harold Hilliard of the *Toronto Star,* Richard Harrington, famous Toronto free-lance photographer and arctic traveler, and Oren Bates of *Western Outdoors* magazine.

There were, occasionally, tokens of esteem. A note from Hudson's Bay House, Winnipeg, in September of 1944, from R.H. Cheshire, after Buffa flew him and Ashley Cooper to the North, read in part, ''I wanted to drop you a line to express our very real appreciation of the fine piloting job you did for us. On a trip such as the one which we just completed we recognize only too well that for safety and success we must depend entirely on the skill and good judgment of our pilot. At no time throughout the trip did we experience the slightest concern. On the contrary, thanks to you, we enjoyed every moment of it. As a small token of appreciation, and also as a reminder of what we hope was for you a very pleasant trip, we are sending you a pair of Hudson's Bay point blankets. These should help you keep warm if again forced down on Boffa Lake!''

But Ernie more than balanced the scales by giving away precious Eskimo artifacts, which could have made him a top collector or a wealthy man. One letter in the files is from N.R. ("Buck") Crump, who was president of the Canadian Pacific Railway when he flew up to Yellowknife for a look at his company's new airline territory. Boffa heard that he collected weapons, and gave his prized Eskimo ivory bow and set of arrows to Grant McConachie so Grant could give them to Crump. But Grant, true to form, gave them to him from Ernie Boffa. Crump wrote to thank Ernie, saying,

> *I do not know of anything that occurred during the entire trip that gave me as much pleasure as receiving this excellent specimen of Eskimo work, and I do appreciate your thoughtfulness.*
>
> *Actually, I got a tremendous surprise immediately I looked at it as it is typical of the design used in the Middle East by the Moslems during the Crusades, and, of course, also of the type used by many of the Oriental tribes. It is a beautiful piece of workmanship and I regard it as being so rare that it is in the classification of a museum piece. . . .*

Boffa also qualified as a Permatelican, B.S., (Restricted) Senior Grade, of the Order of Arctic Experts, established by DEW line crews. The name was coined from Permafrost Expert and/or Radician and/or Mechanic and Tundra Engineer by the boys of the North-Bell system.

Other pieces of parchment he picked up along the way included his 1949 commission as lieutenant in the Reserve Militia, Canadian army, while a member of the Canadian Rangers, #7 Company at Yellowknife. It's a pretty impressive document, bringing greetings from His Majesty, George VI.

He was awarded the Coronation medal by Queen Elizabeth II. He considers this one of his top honors and prizes it with deep feeling.

Occasionally, compensations came in a more unusual form. In the early days at Yellowknife, having had his fill of keeping records in the RCAF, Ernie passed the job over to Nettie and she did his logbooks, when he happened to remember them. A pilot was supposed to enter every load, every stop, every gassing up, and Boffa figured he had more important things to do with the airplane. One day somebody else flew his plane, and discovered the logbook sadly out of date. The jig was up, and E.J.B. was given "five Brownie points" (demerit marks) by CPAir. That was serious!

Then came the night of the fire at the Hudson's Bay store, freezing cold and a wind blowing down on the old Rock, when for hours Ernie and Ted Cinnamon manned the portable pumps, thawed the lines with blow torches, and literally saved all the other buildings which would have gone up in flames, including the CPAir building. So the Brownie points were canceled, and Boffa got a nice letter as well. Justice always triumphs in the end!

— 12 —
THE FLYING BOFFAS

Flying had always been a family affair for Boffa, and three generations later it still is.

Although Katherine Stinson became, in 1918, the first woman pilot to land a plane at Lethbridge, Alberta, Nettie's home town, Nettie Boffa was the first woman to learn to fly there. Not that she had any personal ambitions as a pilot; she did it for Charlie Tweed, who was trying to attract more students in those hungry years, 1935-36. He was such a good instructor and friend that Nettie had few qualms. Besides, she'd watched Ernie, Cec, Charlie and all the other barnstormers risking their necks through the years. She decided E.J.B. wasn't the only member of the family who could sail up, up and away!

But she knew he wouldn't like it, so she took her lessons when he was away from the home field. The first official clue he got was a telegram delivered to him when he was away one day, telling him to get back to Lethbridge in time to celebrate a student's solo flight. There was always a party for your first solo, in those days.

Ernie says he guessed that the party was for Nettie, so he took off from Kindersley, Saskatchewan, and flew home that night, arriving before the party was over. But it wasn't until he had landed and walked into the hangar that he knew for sure it was Nettie who had soloed. It so happened that the aviation inspectors and a bigwig from Ottawa were also at that party, but had left just before Boffa had landed in the dark without regulation lights of any kind. He figured he was in a real jam, because they would see his plane in the morning and wonder when it had arrived! But nothing came of it, for which E.J.B. was thankful.

Nettie never went far enough with her flying to get her license; she said one pilot in the family was enough. But she'd shown Ernie she could do it if she wanted to, and that was the object of the exercise. Her solo brought much-needed publicity to the club and did attract some student instruction fees for Charlie.

Actually the family flying had begun earlier than that. Back in 1929, Ernie's niece, Lea Faro, learned to fly in Great Falls. She made the front page of the *Great Falls Leader* in May of that year, headlined "Boots, Look to Your Records," tying her in with the popular comic strip of the day, "Boots and Her Buddies," in which the blonde heroine, Boots, was also learning to fly.

Ernie admits he really sweated out that solo flight of his student-niece. He knew that if anything happened to Lea, his sister would kill him!

Boffa gave his son-in-law, Gordon ("Smoky") Hornby, his first instruction in 1950 at Yellowknife, then Smoky went on to Edmonton and got his private license. The two were associated in several flying ventures through the years and enjoyed working together. Smoky Hornby moved south to Edmonton and made a career for himself in management of housing projects.

Son Joe Boffa absorbed flying through his pores as a kid in the North, and after the family moved to Los Angeles in 1957, he started flying Taylorcraft there and got his commercial ticket later. Daughter Joan's husband, Gary Hanson, was another of Ernie's pupils, who graduated to flying for PanArctic in the Canadian north. Gary's son Bret is into hang-gliding in Alaska. Through the years, Ernie was usually around to help stake the younger members of the family when it involved planes or flying.

Joe doesn't fly any more. He went to the university and got his Bachelor of Science degree in computer science. Ernie says proudly, "He's going in the front door!"

And what about the founder of the Flying Boffas? When did he pack it away?

Well, Ernie got himself a Taylorcraft down in Los Angeles, just

"I really sweated that one out!" said Ernie on the day, in 1929, his niece Lea Faro made her first solo flight.

ʒreat Falls Leader
"Great Falls—Niagara of the West"

ʒAT FALLS, MONTANA, SATURDAY, MAY 4, 1929. PRICE FIVE CENTS

BOOTS, LOOK TO YOUR RECORDS!

Because Miss Lea Faro, Sparkling Little Great Falls Brunette, Is Out After Them; She's 16, and Ready to Go!

Smoky Hornby, seen here at Great Bear Lodge, had his first flying instruction from his father-in-law — as did Boffa's other son-in-law Gary Hanson.

to keep his hand in, and decided he'd fly out of a field at Compton, the only local airport without radio control, which suited him just fine. He'd had the Taylorcraft completely overhauled, re-bored and all set for more flying time. On the test flight, he took off, climbed up to five hundred feet, ready to make his first turn on the circuit when she quit on him. The engine seized. The prop stopped and there was that sudden, alarming silence.

Boffa looked around. He was over a dump and a school. Then there was a railroad track and some high-tension wires. On the other side there was an old oil well in a small field. That had to be it. So he glided over the tracks, sideslipped under the power line, landed on one wheel while turning, and stopped 20 feet from the oil well.

"Boy! Was I lucky in that field!" he says, shaking his head. "I had to take the plane apart to haul it out of there, but there wasn't a scratch on it."

For some years after moving south, he wintered in Los Angeles and headed North with the birds each spring. He kept busy all summer flying sport fishermen out of Great Bear Lodge, setting up camps, bringing in supplies and moving small boats from one fishing spot to another. He enjoyed it.

But one day he decided that was enough, and closed out his logbooks. They show a total of 20,000 hours, on everything from scheduled airlines to single-engine bush planes. He had carried every type of cargo, from oil drills to corpses, x-ray teams to election ballot boxes. He had earned not only his pilot tickets but engineer's as well. He had his Senior Commerical and Instrument Rating for Transport license. But the old eyes were getting tired and required trifocals (the top section to handle the radio stuff, middle for distance viewing, and bottom for reading the instrument panel).

So, in 1972, he let the licenses lapse and decided he was through flying, except for fun. The medicals, which had been a breeze, were getting stickier as the years went by. Doctors didn't know him personally, as they used to.

"There was a Russian doctor at Big River, I remember," Ernie says with a satisfied nod. "He knew his stuff. He'd just say, 'Well, how do you feel?' And if you said 'O.K.,' that was good enough for him. We had a good doctor in Edmonton for years, too, and we used to say, 'What are we going to do when this guy dies?' "

But there were some medicos who didn't cooperate all that well through the years. There was one, in Yellowknife, for example, who gave him the "whisper test" for his hearing ability one day, which Ernie passed. But when he went down to Edmonton to the Department of Transport to get his card, they told him he hadn't passed the hearing test because the doctor said the room in which it had been conducted was too small! That wasn't very well received by E.J.B.

Then there was a CPAir doctor who checked his eyesight one year and advised him to ask Grant McConachie to give him "a nice ground job." Boffa was livid.

"Ground job!" he roared. "I'll still be flying when you are in your grave, Mister!" And he was.

Fortunately, in 50 years of flying, Ernie never lost or injured a passenger. When asked about that, Boffa just says there were good reasons — it wasn't all luck and it wasn't all skill.

There have been some honors and some publicity through the years. But for Ernie Boffa, sitting relaxed in the comfortable living room of his Westwood apartment, the greatest tribute of them all

Bret Hanson took naturally to flying. His craft in this photo from his Boffa grandparents' collection is only one of his favorites.

came on that day in 1931 when he was flying with Cec McNeal on a barnstorming tour at Nanton, Alberta.

Ernie was at the controls and it was McNeal's turn to make the parachute jump. He had already climbed out on the wing and was hanging onto the front cockpit, ready to jump, when the engine made a horrible sound and stopped. The cylinder had broken.

"All McNeal had to do was jump," Ernie says, still shaking his head in wonder. "But do you know what he did? He climbed back into that plane, just as though it was the safest place in the world, and I guess that's the greatest compliment a man could pay you. And by golly, we got down into a wheat field O.K. I said to him after, 'What the hell's the matter with your head?' "

McNeal had logged some 30,000 flying hours and was chief pilot for CPAir's Pacific region when he died in the 1966 crash of a jet at Tokyo. He was 57.

Are there any places in the Canadian North that Boffa would like to go back to? There are, and one of them is in the Thelon Game Sanctuary. He spotted something from the air, years ago, which looked as if someone might have lived there once and Ernie would sure like to check that out.

In addition, he's got interests in some likely gas and oil properties, which might just be worth something some day, probably in time to help his five grandsons and four great-grandsons. And if they're anything like E.J.B. they'll be heading for the North, the Bush and the places where there are still spots on earth without beer cans and people.

Perhaps, on their way to those places, they'll fly over Boffa Drive in Yellowknife, and remember . . .

Today, there are regularly scheduled air services between Yellowknife and places which once had magic names: Rankin Inlet, Frobisher Bay, Holman Island and Gjoa Havn, Spence Bay and Pelly Bay. A phone call to your travel agent gives you a comfortable, reserved seat to Coppermine or Cambridge Bay in sleek modern aircraft. Times have changed.

Airports, year-round runways, lighted airstrips, telex, radio communications, weather information, efficient new aircraft and communications system, and lots of aviation gas everywhere, make these flights just another day's routine work for pilots today. Most of them have never heard of the pilots who flew without any of those support systems 40 years ago.

As for the DEW line sites, which cost so much in physical effort under cruel arctic conditions — a recent U.S. government policy paper has proposed a major reduction, and recommends using modern radar posts instead. Setting up a string of radar posts to replace the Pinetree Line would cost $200 million to $300 million, whereas improving the old DEW line stations would cost twice as much now. Canada doesn't think much of the suggestion, and expects to maintain the DEW line until space satellites replace them one of these days.

As for those pioneer x-ray surveys — there are modern health centers, nursing stations and hospitals in almost every community across the Far North now. Tuberculosis is far less a scourge than alcoholism, or lung cancer from smoking, or even deafness from the noisy snow machines which have replaced the old dog teams.

Flying ballot boxes to Arctic settlements is commonplace now, and there are more native members in the legislative assembly at Yellowknife than white.

Tourism is now an important source of revenue in the Northwest Territories. In the special summer editions of the Yellowknife papers, there's a list of interesting local place names, most of them right out of Boffa's memoirs: Mitchell Drive, for Alex, the prospector; McMeekan Causeway, for Jock, the promoter-publisher; Norseman Drive, Stinson Road, Fairchild Crescent, Bellanca Avenue, Franklin Avenue, Pilots Lane, Ingraham Trail, Cameron Falls (for Don); McAvoy Road, for Jim, the mining promoter who had lived next door to Ernie; Gerry Murphy arena; and Stanton Hospital for the beloved doctor who came to Con Mine in 1937 and stayed to help build the community. And there is Boffa Drive, "Named after Ernie Boffa, one of the best-known bush pilots of the North in the forties."

Thornton Alexander Tweed said it best, "The finest pilot that ever flew an airplane." Ernie snorts, and wriggles his shoulders, and allows as how "Tweed said that, not me!"

EPILOGUE

When it becomes known that you are writing a book about Boffa, everyone wants to get into the act. Just about everyone who ever flew with him has a story to tell.

Tommy Clark, now living in Whitehorse, read the typed manuscript and chuckled his way through until he got to the pages about himself. Then it was different.

"It wasn't exactly like he tells it," says Clark. "He turned off before we told him to — just as much his fault as mine — but then that was always the way with Ernie. You sure heard about it when you made any mistake — there were times when I could have killed him. One of them was at Long Lake, out by Yellowknife airport. Didn't he ever tell you how I saved his life out there?"

Then he laughed and went back 40 years to the long summer flying hours, lugging heavy oil barrels into and out of floatplanes down at the Yellowknife dock, then up to Long Lake for transfer to other aircraft. Here's the story:

> In those days, the flight mechanic went with the plane. You just worked as long as that aircraft was flying, and you didn't eat or sleep until the flying was all over. You went wherever the plane went, and you could be gone for days at a time without a break.
>
> So when you got a day off, it was something special. We'd been working a long, steady streak that summer and I finally had a day off. So I climbed all those steps up over the Rock to the bunkhouse on top, got out of the filthy, greasy overalls I'd been living in, got all cleaned up, and put on my one and only suit and clean shirt. I was just heading out for a beer and a good meal when someone ran up and said I was to get down to the dock right away — Ernie was waiting.
>
> Mad! I sure was mad. I ran down those steps in my good suit, reached the plane and told him it was my day off. "So what?" he said. "Load that stuff and let's get going."

*Well, we got out to Long Lake, and went to tie up
before off-loading. I was on one side of the plane and
Ernie on the other. I heard him throw the rope across —
a short throw — then splash, into the water. Then cursing.
Then another splash and short throw. More cursing.
Then, a big splash. This time it was Boffa in the water,
not just the rope, and hollering for help — he can't swim!
So I jumped into the lake — good suit and all — to rescue
him and the next thing I know, he's standing up, grinning
at me, the water only up to his waist. Right then, I could
have killed him! I had to fly back to the base, go all the
way up to the cabin and climb back into those old greasy,
smelly overalls and get back down to the dock to take
off again — without even time to eat! And you mean to
tell me he never mentioned that?*

So we phoned to Los Angeles and Tommy said hello. Then Ernie
said, "Remember the day you saved me from drowning at Long
Lake?" And they both laughed across the miles and the memories.

But Tommy Clark wasn't laughing later when he said, "Boffa
was the best bush pilot I ever knew."

Geddes Webster was a young mining engineer working for the
federal government in Yellowknife in the boom days. He turned
up again in Whitehorse in the summer of 1983 as the head of Geddes
Resources Limited, of Toronto. When he heard there was going
to be a book about Boffa, his eyes lit up and the memories started
coming. He took the trouble to look for some old pictures taken
on early flights with Boffa, and wrote from Toronto:

*In the fall of 1948, just before freezeup, Dr. G.C.
McCartney was commissioned to examine and report on
a uranium showing at Hardisty Lake. With great
reluctance Ernie was prevailed upon to make the trip and,
as I remember events, I took this opportunity to check
claims. The days were short so we took off from
Yellowknife before dawn, hoping to be back that night.
The weather worsened as we flew north, but Ernie got
us to the property.*

*We examined and sampled it and returned to the plane
to find Ernie very upset. The weather was dead calm, it
was cold, and the ceiling was closing in. We had no hope
of returning to Yellowknife that night. Ernie decided
quickly that a trapper's cabin was our only hope, so we*

*hopped a few miles to Hottah Lake. We stayed the night
in a very uncomfortable, smelly and cramped atmosphere.*

*In the morning, before dawn, Ernie was beside himself.
The fog was solid and there was a good skim of ice over
the dead quiet lake. He rushed us through breakfast, had
the plane loaded, warmed up, and waited. We waited and
waited until about noon. Ice was forming all the time.
Then there was a whoop and a holler, Garnet and I just
managed to jump aboard, we cast off and Ernie headed
for what he said was a bright spot in the sky. We broke
ice all the way on the takeoff run directly from the dock.*

*The Norseman was lightly loaded so it took off quickly
and we were indeed soon in a bright spot that opened up
to the sunshine above. Certainly Ernie's keen eye, sense
of weather and prompt action saved us from being frozen
in on floats, which was in his mind one of the cardinal
sins of any bush pilot. The ceiling at Yellowknife was
somewhat better. Our landing there was uneventful and
no one was even remotely concerned or interested in our
adventure, partly because Ernie seemed to have the touch
and sense of timing that worked in his favor. We all
accepted it and expected that extra bit of luck with him.*

*The second episode relates to a visit in July 1950 by
Bob Winters, then the federal minister of mines, while
he was visiting the Northwest Territories. As usual the
government in Ottawa demanded the best plane and pilot
for the intrepid party, which included R.H. Winters, Wop
May, Bob Elliott, Yukon member of parliament Aubrey
Simmons, George Prudham, Ernie Boffa and yours truly.
It was, I suppose, like most such trips with a touch down
at Eldorado, Tuk Tuk, Coppermine, Cambridge Bay and
Bathurst Inlet. At each stop there would be handshakes
all around with the selected proper persons, casual talk
and a feeling on the part of the "outsiders" that they were
"seeing" the country and the people.*

*Ernie really ran the trip, organized everyone's discom-
fort, and in his quiet way, with his smile and self-
assurance, brought the dignitaries back elated and content
in the belief that their trip was a great success. The
highlight was a stop at Gunbarrel Inlet, where many large
lake trout were caught. One was prepared and cooked
by Ernie. Everyone enjoyed the master's touch, both in
the air and on the ground.*

In early September 1950, the National Film Board sent

Highlight of the VIP flight in 1950 was trout fishing in Gunbarrel Inlet. In the "intrepid party" are, from left, Winters, May, pilot Boffa, Elliott, Simmons and Prudham, with Geddes Webster at the camera.

an internationally recognized photographer, O. Borradale [Borradale was involved in filming Sanders of the River and Scott of the Antarctic and many other outdoor films], to Yellowknife to obtain documentary material for a film on the Northwest Territories. Ernie was the pilot chosen. After filming at the Reindeer Station they returned to Yellowknife to restock on film and to pick up supplies.

"I joined the group and we went to Aklavik, Coppermine, Cambridge Bay, Bathurst Inlet and the Thelon Game Sanctuary before heading for home with a stop at the Taltheilei Narrows. Ernie was constantly on the lookout for good material for Borradale. Somehow he heard that a musk ox had been taken at Bathurst Inlet, so he arranged for a delay of the skinning and cutting up of the carcass until we arrived.

There Ernie took charge and got everyone to cooperate with Borradale, who took excellent footage of the entire operation. An Eskimo family whose head was a grandmother, and her grandson of 10, were the stars of the film. The boy had killed the musk ox with a bow and arrow.

The bow was made of pieces of horn or bone that had been riveted together and bound at the joints with sinew. The bow string was also sinew, about three feet long. The *arrow was a rather crooked stick from a scrub Barren Lands willow. The tip was a point fashioned from a tin can lashed to the shaft, and the feathering consisted of a single white ptarmigan pinion feather. The boy and his grandmother had spotted the musk ox and he had stalked it and killed it alone.*

The carcass was about a day old when we arrived, but in good shape, and had been brought to Bathurst Inlet in pieces by the tribe. Borradale spent much time in getting close-ups of the whole operation, especially the grandmother holding raw meat strips by her teeth as she worked on pieces with her ulu, *the only instrument for the job.*

As soon as Borradale was done, Ernie packed us back into the Norseman and we headed for the Thelon Game Sanctuary, where he found a large herd of musk ox and forced them into their traditional circle of defense. Borradale was delighted. Ernie turned and twisted the plane to get good close-ups.

Upon returning to Yellowknife, Ernie had enough time left to stop at the newly established fishing camp at Taltheilei Narrows. After several unsuccessful circuits of the low island in the narrows, he said it was time to go. Suddenly there was a strike and a 38-pound lake trout, the largest of the season, was caught right in front of the camera.

Twice on this trip we ran short of fuel, but it wasn't a problem because Ernie had caches of high-octane gas tucked away in all kinds of accessible places, so we simply

Borradale (right) got choice footage at Bathurst Inlet, where a boy (smallest figure) and his grandmother (left) had killed a musk ox.
(Geddes collection)

137

flew to these as required and pumped in the gas and moved on. The ability of Ernie to organize and complete trip after trip was in itself a personal characteristic, but the cooperation he was able to achieve was often not only because it was in the spirit of the North but it was for Ernie.

One other person eager and willing to add to the Boffa book was Gordon Hornby, Kay Boffa's husband, who grew up in Yellowknife, learned to fly with Ernie, and shared many northern experiences with him through the years. His memories are different, again:

> *Bush pilots were the Yellowknife children's heroes and all the kids knew each aircraft and could tell who was flying it. The airplane was the Cadillac of transport, particularly the Noorduyn Norseman, which operated on skis in the winter and pontoons in the summer. Prospectors were making new finds at places such as Gordon Lake, Contact Lake and Indian Lake, and new mines were being planned. The Norseman aircraft was needed in the North; there was no easier way to get men and materials into the many remote locations.*
>
> *The Barren Lands and the Arctic had not been fully mapped, and so the challenge was there to pioneer new air routes. Flying, particularly in the winter, in the Barren Lands is a treacherous task — even now in modern flying times. This is a tundra area of Canada, without tree growth, approximately five hundred thousand square miles defined by a line drawn from Tuktoyaktuk in the Northwest Territories to Churchill, Manitoba, on Hudson's Bay.*
>
> *In the winter white-outs, where the snow-covered earth and sky become all one and a pilot loses his horizon, can cause terror in a person experiencing it for the first time. The Norseman, like all other bush aircraft at that time, was equipped with a basic panel; flight instruments were airspeed indicator, turn and bank, and sometimes an arti-ficial horizon (if it worked). Navigational equipment was a magnetic compass and directional gyro. Nowadays, air-craft with sophisticated instruments and modern aids to navigation make a flight in winter relatively easy. Most communities now have gas caches, weather reports, radio beacons and service for aircraft. All of these benefits were*

nonexistent in 1943, and some later years. A pilot, flying over unmapped areas, had to be a master of navigation, particularly in dead-reckoning flying.

It was just as well if he could also be a good mechanic, able to service and repair his own airplane. Many flights could take a week or more, without radio contact with anyone. Gas was very scarce and once a trip was started, there was no returning to base because of bad weather. A pilot had to "sit down" and know how to survive and look after his passengers in the most extreme conditions, until the weather cleared and the trip could carry on.

Ernie and Nettie Boffa and their children, Kay and Joan [Joe was born later], arrived in Yellowknife in 1943 and adapted quickly to the demands of a new, rugged community. Ernie was made for the North and he began a demonstration of pioneer flying and navigational ability that set the pace for younger pilots.

An adventurer by nature and a perfectionist in everything he tackled, Ernie soon got the attention of most people living in the North; they all had something to do with aircraft, directly or indirectly, and were reliant on it.

Having left the Royal Canadian Air Force while an instructor in the British Commonwealth Air Training scheme, he had tolerated the military discipline only because of a deep loyalty to his country, Canada. Now, he welcomed the freedom of the North.

It would be misleading to suggest that Ernie was undisciplined. He, in fact, was strongly self-disciplined, an essential ingredient to becoming a good bush pilot. The most valued compliments a pilot can get are those from his own peers. I have heard some of these from pilots: "He flies like a bird," "Ernie has done the greatest overall northern flying job of anyone in Canada," "I wouldn't fly with anyone else."

But this is Flo Whyard's story and I think she has grasped the essence of my father-in-law, Ernie Boffa.

ABOUT THE AUTHOR

Florence E. ("Flo") Whyard started her career in journalism in London, Ontario, Canada, where she attended the university. She earned her limited commercial pilot's license there in 1939. Public relations assignments in Toronto, writing for weekly papers in Ontario, and service in Naval Information during World War II preceded free-lance writing and broadcasting for the Canadian Broadcasting Corporation in Yellowknife, Northwest Territories, from 1945 to 1954. After moving to Yukon Territory she was editor of the *Whitehorse Star* from 1962 to 1970. She has also written articles for publications such as *ALASKA®* magazine, *North* magazine, *Life* and *MacLean's*. She served as Canadian editor for *ALASKA®* magazine and *The MILEPOST®* from 1970 to 1974, and again from 1980 to 1981. Her first book was *My Ninety Years,* published by Alaska Northwest Publishing Company in 1976.

Flo left journalism when elected to the Yukon legislature in 1974. She served as minister of Health and Human Resources for the government of the Yukon from 1975 to 1978. A term as mayor of Whitehorse interrupted her writing again. She was recently named to membership in the Order of Canada.

She lives in Whitehorse with her husband, Jim.

Whyard collection